THE

GRUNCH

WHO ATE THE

BOTTOM

LINE!

Bernie Palmatier, P.H.D.*

Illustrations by Paul Rehg

The Grunch Who Ate the Bottom Line
(Secrets to Attitude Control, Happiness and Achieving Goals)

Editor: Judy Lemaster
Graphic Production: Gregory S. Opt
The Graphic Image, Dayton, Ohio

2013 Revised Edition:
ISBN-10: 149357793X
ISBN-13: 9781493577934

* Many years ago I heard as a joke the fact that PHD represents ... well, if a BS degree is BullSh*t and an MS degree represents "More Sh*t" then a Ph.D must mean "Piled Higher and Deeper." Well, since I have been accused from time to time of being a "Bullsh*tter," I determined I should wear it proudly and have the official designation of "P.H.D.", a slightly improved method of spelling that honorary designation. This will also be a test for determining which people are aware of the difference between a Ph.D. and a P.H.D. So, feel free to refer to me as Dr. Palmatier ... I won't object. But I will question something.

Published by AT&S Publishing

DEDICATION

I promised early in my college career at Ohio State University that I would dedicate my first published book to the memory of my best boyhood friend's mother. Her name was Lorene Gard and she passed away on January 4, 1960, the day I began classes as a freshman in Columbus, Ohio.

ENDORSEMENTS

Bernie Palmatier's Grunch and other fabulous characters have performed a miracle. They have wrestled with some difficult principles of life and success, and simplified them so that anyone can understand them … and use them. Wise men have been trying to do the same for centuries.

- Og Mandino, Author/Lecturer

I love the Grunch.

- Dr. Wayne W. Dyer, Author
Gifts from Eykis, Your Erroneous Zones,
Pulling Your Own Strings,
The Sky's the Limit

It looks like you have something here which will appeal to and help many people. At any rate, I certainly hope so.

- Zig Ziglar

Your book is a delight and I think you are a creative, inventive man. Thoroughly enjoyed it and got much from it … I wish you all good fortune.

- Rosita Perez
NMA Speaker of the Year
Author, *The Music is You*

Bernie Palmatier has truly been an inspiration to me. By applying his principles of "Attitude Control," I've been able to make countless positive advances in my career, personal life, and the fulfillment of my dreams, goals and ambitions. Bernie is one of the most intelligent influences that I have ever been privileged to know. My greatest testimonial for "Attitude Control" is that it gave me the courage, knowledge, and determination to do that which I feared most…start my own business. Leaving the comfort zone of a steady paycheck was always a scary thought for me, but by applying "Attitude Control," I was able to do it.

- Brent McKinley, CTF
Founder & President
FitnessResults123.com

TABLE OF CONTENTS

PROLOGUE

In many respects I matured late in life; even puberty kept me waiting! And now, at the age of forty-three I have a son who is just eight years old. As a single parent since he was less than two years of age, I have had the singular (no pun intended) pleasure of reading, rereading, and reading over again his "favorite" bedtime books and stories. Some of their simplistic plots I could tolerate and, even though Walt Disney was one of my boyhood idols, I found myself insulted by Mickey Mouse dressed to look like Merlin, or Robin Hood, or whatever. Sometimes I felt I would throw up if I had to read certain of my son's "favorites" just one more time!

However, I found that I did not abhor the ones written in rhyme, metered and with words twisted and turned just for the fun of it. And so, I offer this "self-help" epic poem in hopes that all adults, but most importantly those with goals, and especially financial and business ones, will enjoy its special lesson more than once. I hope they will share it with their loved ones whom they wish to have a life more full, fulfilling, enjoyable, happy, expansive, etc., etc., than their own.

I currently ply my skills to the training and motivating of Telemarketing people (and, on occasion, field sales people, accountants, engineers, etc.). In the course of my training program I have developed a session I call the "Attitude Control Seminar." I generally introduce this training session with a statement like this: "I'd like to share with you my personal experience with becoming 'born again' on the subject of Self-Help Psychology." I think of my growing belief in the realities of the things that can be accomplished through the power of positive thinking as a kind of born again experience!

While still in college I became a fledgling salesman with a new division of the *Reader's Digest.* There I was, a pre-medicine student, sold on selling by a man I have yet to thank, Mr. Tom Murray. It was Tom who handed me my first self-help book, *Think and Grow Rich* by Napoleon Hill; which I promptly read and cast aside! It was also Tom who uttered three statements that stuck:

1. "Nothing ever happens until somebody sells something!"
2. "Act enthusiastic and you'll be enthusiastic!"
3. "Whatever the mind of man can conceive and believe, it can achieve!"

The first finally made sense when I learned the ideal definition of the word "selling": "*persuading another to your way of thinking.*" The second seemed pure, unadulterated hypocrisy; and the third fell on fertile ground and germinated!

As I mentioned, I cast aside my first self-help publication. It seemed like so much metaphysical propaganda, probably financed by the boss (e.g. Axiom from the "Law of Compensation": "Give service first and ask for remuneration later and it will come!"). Never had any teacher, instructor, or professor mentioned anything about this attitude, positive thinking stuff. It was always knowledge and logic, logic and knowledge. Get that certificate, that sheepskin, if you want to open doors to a wonderful and secure career. (Little did I know about how to handle what I would face when I passed through those doors!) My mind and my heart fought each of the first two or three or four of these publications as each one fell into my hands and my life!

Finally, a very successful young salesman employed by the SCM Corporation in El Paso, Texas, Jim Edens, helped me by demonstration to change my thinking. Jim's greeting was without fail: "Hi! It's a beautiful day!!" It was the day he said it as we greeted one another on a downtown street in the middle of a flash, torrential downpour that really played on my mind. Obviously, the weather had absolutely nothing to do with Jim's "beautiful day." I stood in that storm wondering whether Jim's cheerful attitude could be a part of the explanation for his fabulous success as a salesman? But the rational part of my mind said, "NO!"

Then several more books and another living example named Tony Freeman came into my life; and I started down the path toward "ATTITUDE CONTROL!" Og Mandino in his *Greatest Salesman in the World's* Scroll Marked VI says, "Today I will be master of my emotions!" Isn't every other virtue a subtitle of the concept of controlling our attitudes towards the positive? With control over our attitudes, we will persist when failure seems imminent! With attitude control we will practice the art of loving; we will see ourselves as the "greatest miracle"; we will "live this day as if it is our last"; "laugh at the world"; "multiply our value a hundred-fold"; "act now," and "pray to our God often." Most importantly, we will pay special attention to the Scroll Marked I. That is the Scroll that commits the reader to three readings per day for thirty days each—with the final reading of the day being aloud.

I often ask people if they have heard of or read the book *The Greatest Salesman in the World.* Then I say, "BUT DID YOU DO IT? DID YOU <u>DO</u> THE BOOK?!?" Well, I did the book back in 1969 through 1970. And I thought the "Scroll Marked I" was the most boring, insignificant, trivial, and meaningless one of all! I was filled with anxiety to get on to the next Scroll! Now, with my twenty-twenty hindsight, I see that that particular exercise was probably the most important of all. You see, it establishes the most powerful and necessary habit of all!

It has recently come to my attention that anything we consistently do for a period of three weeks will, in fact, become a habit! With that knowledge I have now come to realize that "Attitude Control" can only be accomplished when we habitually read, listen to, and otherwise subject our minds and hearts to a constant flow of positive-thought-type literature, tapes, seminars, etc.

The Bible says, "As a man thinketh in his heart, so is he!" And that is a fundamental precept of Dr. Maxwell Maltz's preachings and teachings in his revolutionary *Psycho Cybernetics.* The Bible also reads, "Beware the idle word!" With this thought, I admonish my students to determine for themselves what I call psychological "triggers" that effectively act as "mood elevators." These triggers should set off a chain reaction thought process that will result in the speaker's mind counting and recounting his or her blessings and culminating in the old axiom, "I felt bad because I had no shoes until I met the man who had no feet!"

One of my many-fold repeated triggers is, "Hi! It's a BEAUTIFUL day!!!" When I say those words, my mind, in split "nanoseconds," counts my basic blessings, and I realize that a "BEAUTIFUL" day has absolutely nothing to do with the weather! When someone asks me, "How are you?" I always respond with, "Fantastic! And getting better!!!" Now, the first several times I say those words each day, the inflection in my voice belies the meaning of the words; however, by the third, fourth, and fifth repetitions, I begin to sound like I mean what I'm saying, and positive things start to happen inside and outside of me!

I believe people want to do business with people who make them feel better! At the very least they like doing business with people who do not burden them with their problems. Whether we know it or not, the inflection in our voices can tell people, "I've got many and serious problems. Won't you share them with me and let me tell you all about them?" In other words, we

9

have a little "self-pity party" almost instantaneously in the inflection used on the one-word response, "Fine." Don't do that! Misery loves company, but company doesn't love misery. So, if you want to be alone, simply tell people exactly how miserable you are, and you'll be miserable alone!

Good things come to those who think and dwell upon good thoughts! It works! Everyone can truly share in the bounty provided by this great free enterprise system, this great country, this great world in which we all live! Have faith, believe, fill your Spiritual Well on a daily basis; start your personal Attitude Control program now; and watch your lifestyle, career, goals, interpersonal relationships, virtually every aspect of your life, grow and improve!

YOU CAN DO IT IF YOU WILL!!!

THE GRUNCH

WHO ATE THE

BOTTOM LINE!

by Bernie Palmatier

Illustrations by Paul Rehg

THE GRUNCH WHO ATE THE BOTTOM LINE!

Things were fine; the sun did shine;

Business was bright on both sides of the line.

People were smiling! Oh yes they were!

Things looked Great! Yes Ma'am, yes Sir!

The humans who worked there, whether standing or seated,

Burst forth with cheer toward everyone they greeted!

On the phone or in person, it mattered not,

From that well of enthusiasm, out it shot:

"Good morning, Hello, It's a beautiful day!!!

"How may I help you? Just name the way!

"With this cheerful greeting I'm trying to say,

"We love you and your business—don't go away!"

"Service and quality, that's our creed!

"Service and quality with the utmost of speed!

The best of the best, that's what we give,

"Around our company it's the way we live!

"Nobody knows what gave it the start,

"But everyone knows it comes from the heart!

"It always has and it always will,

"Our job enjoyment shows in the till!

"We don't dread Mondays or the starting hour,

"Our job assignments don't make us sour,

"Wednesdays for most are considered the hump,

"Even Fridays and weekends don't make us jump!

"We like what we do and we do what we like,

"Ready! Set! Hut one! And hike!

"Each does his part to carry the ball,

"Cause we're a team, one and all!

"We know it takes our best to beat

"That other team just down the street.

"Managers and workers in whatever amount,

"Titles don't matter, titles don't count,

"We just know that the security we feel,

"Has never been false, it's really real.

"And doing the best that we can do,

"Makes things great for me and for you!"

19

So the widgets and gidgets and warbles they made

Were quality ones in the sun and the shade.

When meetings were held, ideas would flow,

And their little company would grow and just grow!!

With mutual respect, associates they were,

Equal parts to the whole, the him and the her!

And so it was, for many short years,

Free from the doubts and free from the fears,

The doubts and the fears that one often hears,

From friends and from neighbors and newspapers and peers;

The ones that teach such negative lessons,

The ones often born of economic recessions,

Where sales go away and business turns down,

And even the sun comes up wearing a frown!

Well suddenly, methinks, 'twas a Monday or Tuesday.

Or was it a Friesday? No, no! 'Twas a Throosday!

Silently it came like a cat or a dog;

Quietly, stealthily, just like a fog!

Slowly, but slowly it crept through the place,

Enveloping each at its own snaily pace.

The first little sign was when Suzy who

Answered the phone and said, "Who are YOU?"

With inflection that wasn't quite like it should,

That caused a reaction that wasn't all good!

The caller it seems was rightly offended,

And moments later the relationship ended!

With shock and dismay Suzy turned to her neighbor,

Who just happened to be Ms. Nancy Faulhaber:

"Nancy," she said, with a quizzical look,

"I didn't say what I should, I didn't do what it took!

"That wasn't like me to respond that way!

"Oh well, it must be just 'THAT KIND OF DAY.'"

You know, "JUST ONE OF THOSE DAYS" when you break a lace,

And for twenty-four hours you're last in each race.

"JUST ONE OF THOSE DAYS" when an attempted warble comes out a wobble,

"JUST ONE OF THOSE DAYS" when a formerly fleet step turns out a hobble!

"JUST ONE OF THOSE DAYS" that started so bright,

Where things turned wrong, nothing went right!

"JUST ONE OF THOSE DAYS" where an early event,

Was a precursor of things to be sent;

Where the horoscope, mirror, or lace foretold,

Our actions should be anything but bold!

And sure enough, just like you thought,

The day was a bummer, you got what you ought!

From morning to night things got wrong and then wronger,

And instead of a short day it got longer and longer!

But Suzy was bothered from early 'til lunch,

She never suspected, she had nary a hunch,

That there in the corner in a little 'ol bunch,

Crouched that mean little, voracious little, line-eater we call–

Now when the Grunch first starts he can hardly be seen.

He starts out mild, but grows steadily mean!

Some can see him, but most cannot,

He goes from cool to very red hot!

And things will go from good to not very right,

When he satisfies his huge, as in LARGE, appetite!!

He starts with that size, which as I've mentioned is smaller,

And grows with each bite 'til he becomes much taller!

He's such a rogue, a rascal, a bounder!!

Each bite that he gets makes him rounder and rounder!!

Each bite, you say, sounds like a rut!

Each bite, you say, each bite of the what?

Say what! Say what! Oh! That's just fine!!

Say what! You say, each bite of the line?

The line, you say! What line, you say?

Why, the line we work to create each day!!

The ONE with which we measure results,

The ONE the entire world consults,

The ONE that tells if we've done our work,

That makes us proud or makes us shirk,

The ONE that all our efforts come right down to,

The ONE we often smile or frown to:

THE BOTTOM LINE!

THE BOTTOM LINE! Comes the call!

THE BOTTOM LINE! THE BOTTOM LINE!

That says it all!!!

Now the Grunch in the end can eat it all!

Right to the end he has a ball!

Sans care or taste, the pit or the pulp,

He starts with the nibbles, never a gulp!

With nibbles and dribbles and quibbles and help,

In come the "NEGGIES" with a Yip! and a Yelp!

The Neggies are friends of the Grunch they say;

Their skimpering and scampering only looks like play,

But they're slaves to the Grunch that don't go away,

Slaves to the Grunch who have come to stay!

Slaves, I say! Slaves to the Grunch,

Slaves who bring him something to munch,

Bits and pieces of the line to eat,

The line, you know, his favority treat!

They perch on your shoulder, left or right,

And scream they do with all of their might,

Something bad, something not good,

To make you think what you oughtn't should!

And since they're sitting so awfully near,

One or the other of a human ear,

A negative thought will definitely enter,

And center itself right in the center,

Of the human brain, that wonderful shelf

That causes the good or the bad for itself,

So Suzy, poor Suzy couldn't hear nor see,

That ugly old Neggie perched so darn close to me!

Nor the one dressed up all bright and fancy,

Perched on the shoulder of her co-worker, Nancy!

Nor the ones that had taken much of the space,

On shoulders of people all over the place!!!

So when Nancy came back from lunch, as it were,

She said to him, or was it a her?

"What a lousy break, the food was bad!

"The waitress was slow, the cook was a cad!

"Now I don't feel like working, so I don't think I will!

"This day is a downer, so it's time that I'll kill!!"

But that wasn't like her, I promise you, sir,

That wasn't like her, fer shur, fer shur!

Efficient and prompt with the filing and letters,

From clock in to clock out she got better and betters.

But that darn old Neggie, perched as it was,

Gave her a ring, gave her a buzz,

That made her normal up to a down,

Her smile flipped over, now 'twas a frown!

Now as the time went by, I'm sad to say,

Things got worse with each passing day,

Until even the office manager, Marge,

Got down on the troops, by and large:

"C'mon, get busy! What's wrong with you all?

"You're not doing your parts to carry the ball!

"Let's cut the breaks and the goofing around,

"Get your nose to the grindstone, your ear to the ground!"

"WORK! WORK! WORK!" screamed the Neggie there.

Seems he'd got twisted in Marge's hair.

"WORK! WORK! WORK!" and "What's so funny?"

"Ya gotta work hard to earn yer money!!!"

Where Marge was once the encouraging one,

Now she made work the reverse of fun.

And Sam the salesman par excellence,

Oft times made the entire difference,

Between the 'his' and 'their's' of the competition;

Enthusiasm rang in each repetition!

Customers knew that if problems arose,

Sam would be there right on the nose,

With a smile and the service they'd grown to expect,

The kind that earns the customer's respect.

Sam had always made calls as a cheerful dude,

But this time must have been a **GOOO, BLOOO** mood!

The weather was great, 'twas a gorgeous day,

there was no way to doubt it!

But the Neggie caused Sam to respond in this cynical way,

"What's so beautiful about it!"

Even Carl the accountant and his bookkeeper, too,

And Paul the plant manager and his foremen knew,

That something eerie was in the air,

Neggies were here, Neggies were there,

Neggies, Neggies, everywhere!

In the offices, warehouses, and on the shipping docks,

Their wonderful business was on the rocks!

Who could save it? What could they do?

They had to try something new!!!

Finally Bill, the head of sales and one of the sages,

Saw the ad on the business pages.

SINESS PAGES

SEMINAR TODAY ON...
ATTITUDE CONTROL !!

"IF YOUR ORGANIZATION IS DEEP IN A HOLE,
ATTEND THIS SEMINAR ON "ATTITUDE CONTROL"!
IN YOUR SITUATION YOU CAN'T BORROW, STEAL, OR BEG,
HOW'ERE THERE IS A SOLUTION TO THE QUESTION
OF CHICKEN AND EGG.

MOST HAVE IT BACKWARDS, SO YOU MAKE THE SWITCH,
GET A POSITIVE ATTITUDE AND THEN YOU'LL GET RICH!!!
IT TAKES HARD WORK TO MAKE IT WELL,
BUT IF YOU'LL PUT FORTH THE EFFORT,   YOUR PRODUCTS WILL SELL!
SO SPREAD THE WORD, IT'S ALMOST LIKE MAGIC,
WITHOUT THE "POZZIES" THE RESULTS CAN BE TRAGIC!
BERNIE'S MY NAME AND "UP'S" MY GAME!
COME MEET THE POZZIES IF IT'S ALL THE SAME
TO YOU AND YOUR COMPANY, YOUR JOB AND YOUR LIFE,
ESSEN THE STRESS AND COPE WITH THE STRIFE,
AT COMES WITH THE TERRITORY WE ALL CALL EARTH.
OMISE YOU'LL TAKE HOME YOUR MONEY'S WORTH!!!"

SEMINAR TODAY ON …
ATTITUDE CONTROL!!

"If your organization is deep in a hole,

Attend this seminar on 'Attitude Control!'

In your situation you can't borrow, steal, or beg,

How're there is a solution to the question

Of chicken and egg.

*Most have it backwards, so **YOU** <u>make the switch,</u>*

*Get a positive attitude and **THEN** you'll get rich!!*

It takes hard work to make it well,

But if you'll put forth the effort,

Your products will sell!

So spread the word, it's almost like magic,

Without the "Pozzies" the results can be tragic!

Bernie's my name and "up's" my game!

Come meet the Pozzies if it's all the same

To you and your company, your job and your life,

Lessen the stress and cope with the strife,

That comes with the territory we all call earth.

I promise you'll take home your money's worth!!!"

So Bill did go and learn he would,

How to replace the bad with the good!

How the mind so similar to the computer functions,

How he had to learn to control its crazy compunctions,

To react in the negative toward the things it encounters

To accept without question the words of the doubters.

He learned how the "G" in "GIGO," "Garbage In, Garbage Out,"

Can be changed to "GOOD" if you're careful about

The things you read and listen to,

The things you think, the all-important who,

You allow to form the type of "company you keep,"

'Cause these are the seeds of the harvest you'll reap!

And he heard this Bernie, this speaker, this guide,

Talk about taking the "Pozzies" and their lessons inside,

To fill and to fuel the mind, and the heart as well,

To fill and to fuel "THE SPIRITUAL WELL";

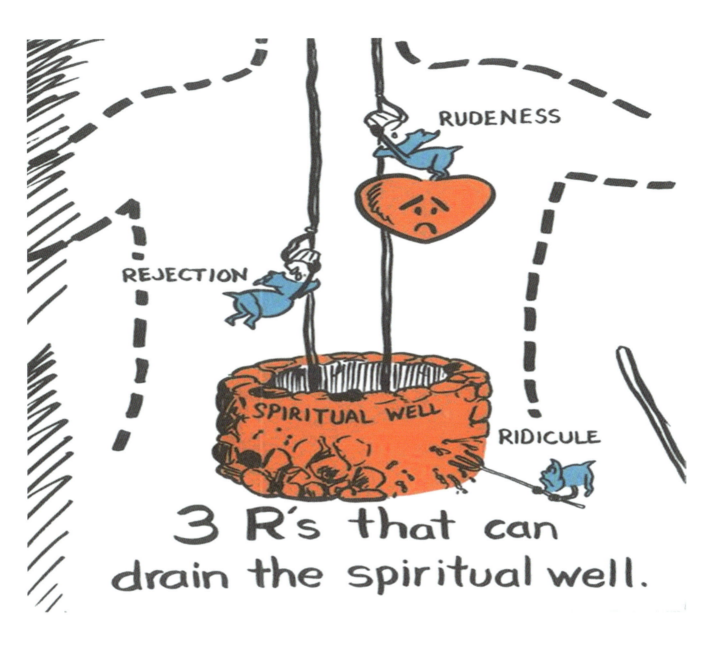

RUDENESS

REJECTION

SPIRITUAL WELL

RIDICULE

3 R's that can drain the spiritual well.

The WELL that goes empty and makes life a Hell,

When the world won't buy whatever you sell.

He spoke of how happiness left neglected,

Slips away slowly and undetected,

And in come the Neggies so unexpected,

By the mind and the heart left unprotected!

"You know," he said, "We begin to talk

Long before we even learn to walk!

This ain't the exception, it's the norm,

The second word most come to form,

Right after 'da,da,' I'm sure you'll agree,

Is 'no,' and 'no, no,' just look and see!

And soon it's 'WOULDN'T' and 'COULDN'T,' 'SHOULDN'T' and
'DON'T!'

And 'STOP IT!' and 'DROP IT!' and 'ISN'T' and 'WON'T!'

Soon we're conditioned in a negative way,

With thoughts for work and even thoughts for play!

And the more we practice the easier 't will be,

To react the opposite of positively!"

"You see, the things you say affect the things you think,

Thoughts that fly much more quickly than a wink!

Special words you must pick that I call 'TRIGGERS,'

Words that…'Yep! That's right! Uh huh. It figgers…

Cause the speaker to automatically count,

His or her blessings in whatever amount.

And those bullet-like thoughts should fly to a target you'll find so neat:

'I FELT BAD 'CAUSE I HAD NO SHOES

'TIL I MET THE MAN WHO HAD NO FEET!'

And those I call 'VERBAL MOOD ELEVATORS' that work over and over each day,

'BEWARE THE IDLE WORD' and choose carefully those you repeatedly say!"

"So I suggest you meet and get to know well,

My friends the 'Pozzies' and the program I sell!

The Pozzies have names and encouragement galore,

Most can be found in your local bookstore!

They're friends you can count on, they won't let you down,

I can promise you'll feel like you're wearing a crown!

So whatever your station, whatever your role,

The Pozzies can help you achieve your goal!"

"Now the pozzie "Mandino' looks like a rabbit.

He can help develop that wonderful habit

Of reading and rereading and reading aloud

Thoughts and principles that'll make you proud,

Ones that can lead to hard-earned success,

Ones that can help with your happiness!

You'll take your place with those few other souls,

When you absorb what is taught in those ten little scrolls!!!

And that old Pozzie Doc Maltz comes like an owl,

Not with a screech and not with a howl,

But just as expected of that wisest of birds,

He shares cybernetics in the simplest of words;

Something not new beneath the sun,

But ways you, too, can have more fun,

With work on your image, what you think of yourself,

68

And if that ain't enough, then look to the elf.

Schuller he's called, Schuller that's all,

"Possibility Thinking" sends you right up the wall!

You'll learn how he and others thought to improve THEIR station,

How "GREAT PEOPLE ARE ORDINARY ONES WITH

    EXTRAORDINARY AMOUNTS OF DETERMINATION!!"

And that Pozzie Emerson, by 'Ralphie' he's known,

May the seeds of his writings forever be sown!

"Self Reliance," the essay, will open your mind,

Oh! The wonders of 'Self Help' I'm sure you'll find!

And the Pozzie named Peale, and Ziglar, too,

Can help to make YOU believe in YOU!

Clason and Carnegie and Buscaglia and Waitley,

Can prevent you from being a "Johnny-Come-Lately"!

The Nightingales, Frankls and all the Girards,

Insure that you're holding all of the cards.

Yes, there's even a Pozzie called JESUS, my friend!

And here's just one powerful message he wanted to send:

"I CAME THAT YOU MIGHT HAVE LIFE

AND HAVE IT MORE ABUNDANTLY," (John 10:10)

He didn't say it once, but most redundantly:

"IF YOU HAVE BUT THE FAITH OF A MUSTARD SEED…"

(Matt. 17:20)

Just name your desire, just speak your need.

He said, "SEEK YE FIRST THE KINGDOM OF HEAVEN," too,
And "YOU'LL FIND IT EXISTS WITHIN EACH OF YOU!!!" (Luke 7:21)

"Now the Pozzies you've heard me speaking of,
All mentioned the winning power called 'LOVE,'

A 'FORCE' so strong that when sustained each day,

Is guaranteed to chase and keep the Neggies away!"

But Bill was shocked when Bernie said:

"These things must be read and then 'REE, REREAD';

'Cause there is no such things as 'self-motivation,'

Self Discipline's the watch word for maintaining your station!

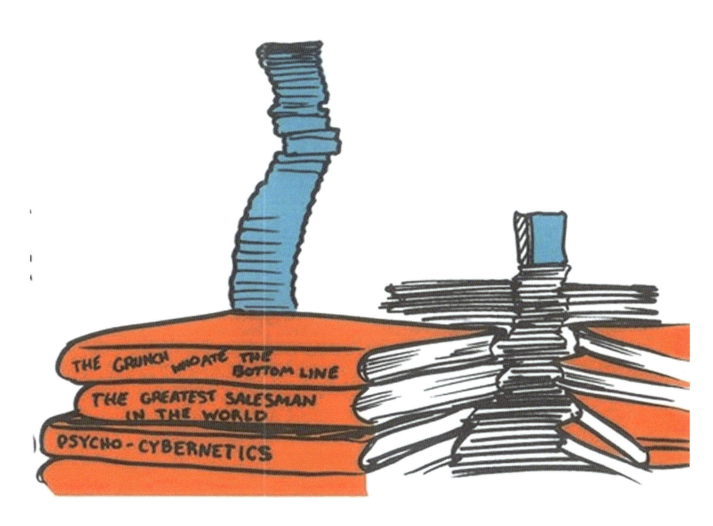

Every day of the world not just one or two!

Seven days a week or MORE WILL DO!

Set aside that time for preventative medicine,

It takes sheer will and SELF DISCIPLINE!

And let it be known and understood,

It's all the harder when times are good!

And in the beginning even three times a day

May not be enough to push the neggies away!

(So study the board and the things I have writ,

Motivation to discipline is a fringe benefit!)

"But persist if you will, keep sight of your goal,

And watch for that change in your very own soul!!

Every day, each day you fight to sustain,

The 'GIGO' rule will help you maintain,

A smile on your face and a warmth in your heart,

Throughout each day you look forward to start!!

So begin tomorrow…NO! BEGIN RIGHT AWAY!!!

HEED THESE WORDS I'VE CHOSEN TO SAY!!

Sink them deep into your subconscious soul,

And I promise you'll have "ATTITUDE CONTROL!!"

So Bill carried them back to the office next morning!

Those mean little Neggies were caught with no warning!

Pozzies got to work and I mean post haste!

They simply had no time to waste!

They chased and chased, and chased and chased

'Til the last little Neggie was out of the place!

And it didn't take long I have a hunch,

Until they were followed by that fat, old Grunch!

So remember, my friends, if you think of rejection,

You'll get what you thought, there is no exception,

You'll get what you think, it's what you expect,

Those negative thoughts you've got to reject!

So check left and then right and all through your hair,

JUST TO BE SURE A POZZIE IS WHAT'S SITTING THERE!!!

OBJECTIFIED WILL

"The most important factor in building an excellent football strength and conditioning program is will power!!!
Intellect tires…The Will, never!
The Brain needs sleep, the Will, none!
The Whole body is nothing but objectified will!"
  -   **Tom Landry, Coach**
      Dallas Cowboys professional football team

The jack held the automobile suspended several feet above the ground. Suddenly, unexpectedly, it fell, pinning the man working on it beneath its two tons of steel and iron! The lady standing nearby weighed less than one hundred and twenty-five pounds. Yet, due to the flow of adrenalin, she was able to lift the car so that the pinned man was able to crawl or be pulled out from under with minimal injury!

Such cases of superhuman achievement, attributable to the flight or fright releasing of the powerful hormone adrenalin, are numerous. They are almost too astounding to be believable!

Therefore:

WARNING! DO NOT READ THIS DISSERTATION ON OBJECTIFIED WILL UNLESS YOU PRESENTLY HAVE A BURNING GOAL AND WOULD LIKE TO ACHIEVE IT MORE QUICKLY AND MORE ASSUREDLY THAN IF YOU WERE TO LEAVE IT TO CHANCE OR TO NORMAL HUMAN CAPABILITIES!!!

TO THE ORGANIZATION AND ITS LEADERS:

Mr. Mark Rednick gave me the greatest gift one man can, I believe, give another. In addition to conditioning me toward a positive way of looking at everything, Mark issued me what I now refer to as "THE THREE WEEK CHALLENGE." This work-related Challenge became a gauntlet that I successfully maneuvered, and my life was forever altered. He is also to be credited with creating the environment conducive to "over-achievement" and even "super-achievement!" As a result, he made me an addict to the euphoric feeling exemplified in this pearl of wisdom that Ralph Waldo Emerson so eloquently committed to posterity in his essay, "Self Reliance":

"A man is relieved and gay when he has put his heart into his work and done his best; anything else he says or does shall give him no peace!"

Another quote upon which I based this short dissertation is from Thomas Peters and Robert H. Waterman's best-selling book, *In Search of Excellence (Lessons from America's Best Run Companies):*

"The success of any organization will always be a direct result of the effectiveness of first level supervision."

A third quote is from a *Sixty Minutes* segment featuring the highest ranking woman in the United States Navy and the creator of Cobol Computer programming language some three or four decades ago: "The major problem we have in both the public and private sectors is management! Management is a term derived primarily from the financial community, and is an accurate term when being applied to debits, credits, ledgers and other inanimate objects. It was never meant to be used when referring to the accomplishing of tasks by people. What we need in this country are schools that teach the lost, but much needed, art of leadership! People were meant to be LED, NOT MANAGED!"

The fourth quote I feel most significant to this essay comes from my own rude awakening: "THE WORK ETHIC IS DEAD OR DYING; LONG LIVE GOAL-ORIENTED MOTIVATION!" No longer does the American worker give it everything he or she has got to give, and take pride in the results simply because "that's the way Dad and Granddad did it," or because, "that's just the way it's always been done." People want and need more of a purpose in their lives, and, ultimately, in their careers.

88

Mark used to say, "Remember one thing: this is a free country and nobody HAS to work for anybody; they have to want to!" He also often repeated another unalterable fact of business: "Everyone will be successful working somewhere! The question is, will it be for you or your competitor? The entire difference is a matter of your effectiveness as a trainer and leader—and our ability to create an environment in which he (or she) can grow to realize his (or her) full potential!"

I have often said, "I believe in the rehabilitation of all smokers, drug addicts, criminals, mediocre performers, and failures!" I also believe in the rehabilitation of all ineffective first-level supervisors. I, personally, deny the existence of a term we often hear applied to certain individuals in every profession: "BURNOUT!" I contend there is no such condition! Dr. Robert Schuller prefers to call it "Brownout." I call it the "Batting Slump." In either event, the underlying premise is that the down cycle in any field of endeavor is temporary—NOT TERMINAL! My contention is, especially regarding my chosen career, that there is no such thing as "burnout;" there are simply poorly trained and under-motivated, under-incentivized, and under-compensated people! The length of the "slump" is entirely a factor of the attention paid, and effectiveness of, a sensitive, well-equipped first-level supervisory staff! So often supervisors actually apply what I call "cattle-prod"-type techniques that actually reduce employee performance, and act to deepen and lengthen the slump.

I would like to emphasize the importance of a short, specific section of *In Search of Excellence,* and hope every manager (leader) hears the revolutionary nature of what is being said:

> Positive reinforcement also has an intriguing Zen-like property. "It nudges good things onto the agenda instead of ripping things off the agenda." Life in business, as otherwise, is fundamentally a matter of attention–how we spend our time. Thus management's most significant output is getting others to shift attention in desirable directions (e.g. "Spend more time in the field with customers").
>
> There are only two ways to accomplish such a shift. First, we attempt through positive reinforcement to lead people gently over a period of time to pay

attention to new activities. This is a subtle shaping process. Or we can "take the bull by the horns" and simply try to wrestle undesirable traits off the agenda (e.g. "Quit staying in the office filling in forms").

Skinner's argument is that the wrestler's approach is likely to be much less efficient, even though it may not seem that way in the very short run. That is, ripping items off an agenda leads to either overt or covert resistance: "I'll get out of the office, if you insist, but I'll spend the time in the local pub." The "nudge it on the agenda" approach leads to a natural diffusion process. The positively reinforced behavior slowly comes to occupy a larger and larger share of time and attention. By definition, something (who cares what?) less desirable begins to drop off the agenda. But it drops off the agenda on the basis of our sorting process. The stuff that falls off is what we want to push off in order to make room for the positively reinforced items. The difference in approach is substantial. If, by force of time alone (a non-aversive force), we choose to push a low-priority item off, then it is highly unlikely that we will cheat on ourselves and try to do more of the less attractive (just pushed off the agenda) behavior. So, back to Zen: THE use of positive reinforcement goes with the flow rather than against it.

Our general observation is that most managers know very little about the value of positive reinforcement…

Talk about your glaring example of the gross understatement! I marvel at the lack of exclamation points in the original text! I'm sure that a majority of "managers" will be shocked and feel indicted, and somewhat defensive, when they see their daily modus operandi so blatantly attacked! We are at the zenith of a human relations revolution that began approximately two decades ago. Those leaders of people in the business environment who are unable to see the light and make the transition will find themselves, and their careers, lost!

It takes only common sense for one to realize that the only people potentially more important than first level supervisors are first level employees, period, who actually implement all the great schemes and dreams of the "managers" theorizing in the conference rooms and "Ivory Towers" of the corporation. My contention is that the first-level supervisor is primarily needed in the temporary capacities of job function trainer and "short-term goal-oriented motivator" until the individual employee achieves a consistent level of "Attitude Control." "One-Minute Management" (errr, "leadership") techniques will do nicely during the transition period from new employee (trainee) to full-fledged "Attitude Control" disciple.

Megatrends, by Mr. John Naisbitt, predicts a veritable explosion in the arena of "Self Help Psychology" in the latter part of the 20th century. The demand for seminars, books, tapes, etc., on this subject called motivation will expand dramatically, he says. IBM and thousands of other American businesses spend millions of dollars on training. I venture that little of it is dedicated to the training of supervisors on the art of motivating others with a positive mindset to the dove-tailing of personal employee goals into the corporate (or organizational) goals. Little emphasis is placed on the fact that supervisors are, in fact, salespeople who have an obligation to discover the "Hot Button" for each of their charges and then help sustain an over-achiever level of performance by constantly refocusing the employee's sights on his or her personal goals.

This revolution of which I have spoken—"The Human Relations Revolution"—is of such importance that I believe, without proper emphasis, this country could, in fact, ultimately be reduced to a second-rate status in the world economy! We must, as Alvin Toffler points out in *The Third Wave,* see people not as liabilities, but as our GREATEST ASSETS! The Japanese made the transition some time ago. We must make it now! The productiveness of the American worker is on the skids, and the slope is down! Technology has been able to take up much of the slack for several decades; however, as we move to an information processing/high technology economy, the creative, effective productive performance of the individual American worker will be coming into sharper focus. And old-fashioned, "cattle-prod"-type directing of the individual will no longer act to increase productivity or creativity! One Minute Management techniques, exercise programs, out-placement programs, etc. are, I believe, steps in the right human relations direction.

Another projection by Mr. Naisbitt, mentioned in *Megatrends,* is the fact that upwards of fifteen million people will be employed or self-employed and working out of their homes. These people must, of necessity, be accomplished at the principles and practices of "Attitude Control," or they will simply fail; and the movement to individualism and entrepreneurship will be counter-productive!

And so I offer the following:

"Until we believe that the expert in any particular job is most often the person performing it, we shall forever limit the potential of that person in terms of both his contribution to the organization and his personal development..."

-- Quoted in *In Search of Excellence*
Mr. Rene McPherson, Chairman
Dana Corporation

TO THE INDIVIDUAL:

It is an old adage that "a goal is not a goal until it is written down." Most people don't have goals let alone perform the exercise of writing them down on paper! However, I believe the carrot on the stick can be the solution to outstanding performance for the individual who desires a lifestyle that can only be afforded by being an over-achiever.

"Desire, when harnessed, is power." I don't know who said or wrote that, but I know it's true. I do know that Emerson said, "Do the thing and you shall have the power to do it." He said, "Do your thing and I shall know you; do your work and you shall strengthen yourself." Also true! I think he was speaking to all people and especially to all entrepreneurs and/or would-be entrepreneurs.

I was having a talk with a friend of mine who happens to be an S.M.I. (Success Motivation Institute) distributor. What he had to say about goal setting was corroborated by a short discussion I had with a psychologist. The process of "wishing" is an important step in goal setting! First, it's a wish, wishes become dreams, then they become wants, then needs, and then they become prioritized according to our capability to acquire them. But most of us stop at the wishing stage by convincing ourselves that "it's only a wish and wishes don't come true." But the concept of "imaging" written about by Dr. Maxwell Maltz in *Psycho Cybernetics* is nothing more than the practice of firming up a wish until it becomes a believable desire and then a want. It works! I challenge you to think back on something you have wanted in the past, something that your logical, conscious mind told you that you could not afford but that you successfully acquired. You'll find you have already used the concept of "imaging!"

Having a goal that becomes a "burning desire" means having an objective, a purpose, that gives our daily job function meaning. Dr. Victor Frankl discusses the power of a "purpose" in psychotherapy (logo-therapy) in his book *Man's Search for Meaning*. He also helps us with overcoming fears and, ultimately, "Attitude Control" when he teaches the effective use of reverse psychology on the self.

Many of the "self-help" books and authors mention the powerful effects of "Self-Talk" and, most importantly, repetitive Self-Talk. Self-Hypnosis? Subliminal, subconscious programming? Call it what you will, it is an important process in the establishing and achieving of goals!

Given a fixed goal, I believe that (and here's the part that will freak you out!) it is humanly possible to fabricate the flow of that powerful chemical (hormone) adrenalin to effect the focusing of our mental skills toward the successful accomplishing of any task.

As athletes, I and other members of the team met in the restroom just before the start of the big game to "take that last nervous one," even if we had done so minutes before the coach said, "Let's go!" Professional performers talk about how their performances do not go well if they aren't experiencing some nervousness just prior to "going on." I'm sure that performance, especially the possibility of peak performance, is enhanced by the advent of adrenalin.

I have often used the phrase "getting up on my 'psych'" when I talk about my preparation for giving a speech, for an important selling situation, for an extended period of outbound telephone dialing activity, etc. I have described the difficulty of "coming down off my 'psych'" at the completion of one of the above functions, so that I can assume the mindset proper to completing the paperwork or doing the planning necessary for tomorrow's tasks. When I attempt to write while still "pumped up," I notice my hands trembling, as well as other symptoms of adrenalin coursing through my system!

Due to my experience in the personnel recruiting field, I used to point out that the primary message of a college degree was that it was a goal set and met. I now believe that one important discipline installed, due primarily to the "cramming" process, is the "Crisis Complex." I have often said, and heard said by other college graduates, "I function better under pressure and in a crisis situation!" I believe I became a "Crisis Creator" that, when coupled with a highly desirable goal, caused me to function at peak level daily for an extended period of time. And I am convinced that adrenalin comes into play!

I found that adrenalin could also cause what I, in my layman's attempt to communicate this phenomenon, call a mental "Time Warp!" I have experienced this "time warp" when aware that I am about to be involved in an incident that could cause me severe injury. For example, I was a passenger in an automobile when I saw the other vehicle about to impact the very spot where I was sitting. That hurtling vehicle seemed to slow down to "Super Slo-Mo," the car I was riding in spun for what appeared to be tens of minutes, and my friend fell from the open passenger door, his head bouncing slowly on the pavement! Even the sounds of metal on metal and the thud of Jerry's head were slowed as though emanating from a speaker on a jammed tape recorder. I was calm through the entire incident, and took defensive action only to have the typical shock reaction shortly after the danger was removed.

It was, and is, this heightened state of mental awareness that I was able to focus intensely on the mental movie screen located on the interior of my forehead! Mark often repeated the necessity of hearing (and LISTENING TO) what our client or prospect was saying and the necessity of using what he called "Turn On," not "Turn Off," words! As strange as this may seem, when I was "going with the flow (probably of adrenalin!)," I was able to mentally image spelled "operative" words approaching me slowly. These words I would analyze for their connotative meanings looking for the prospect/client's "Hot Button." I would then mentally image my potential response and its operative words moving slowly across the screen. I would weigh their potential impact and effectiveness, evaluate their relationship to the selling process, and, if they struck me as "Turn On," use them. To this day, I work on Teleselling with my eyes closed. But are they really?

This "psyching up" process is key to functioning with heightened mental skills. And I think it begins with "THE FEAR OF FAILURE!" The Bible says, "The beginning of wisdom is the fear of the Lord!" I believe that adrenalin released is a result of the survival instinct, the desire to win, to overcome. But isn't it actually born of the innate, animal instinct to survive? So, before every motivational speech I give, prior to each selling situation, at the beginning of every day that I apply myself to achieve my short, medium, and long-range goals, I run from "Failure!" I control and channel this powerful chemical produced by my body into constructive effort! And it appears to the outside world as enthusiasm!...excitement!...electricity! I "Act Enthusiastic" so that I, ultimately, "Feel enthusiastic"! It works for ME and it can work for YOU!

Define your goals, psych yourself every day of your life, image your success, AND IT WILL BE!

HOW TO DO THE "GRUNCH" ATTITUDE CONTROL PROGRAM

People look at this book and say, "How cute!" or, "It looks like a children's book" or, "I'll bet you're having fun with it!" All of the above are true; it is cute, it is a fun way to introduce yourself to the concept of positive thinking and Self-Help Psychology, and, yes, I am having fun sharing my program for staying "up" with other people. However, this book is also "HEAVY" due to the fact that it asks the readers to MAKE A LIFETIME COMMITMENT TO AN "ATTITUDE CONTROL PROGRAM" largely of their own design. Therefore, the book is more so a "System," and requires that certain exercises be performed and a definite procedure followed, in order to complete the initial reading of the book. That procedure and those exercises are as follows:

1. On your first reading of the book, do as you do with most books and read from the beginning to the end, relax and enjoy. However, on your second reading, go to the outside of the back cover of the book (or the last position in the eBook) that explains the retention and recall power of "jingles" in the advertising industry. When I conduct seminars, I have found that fully fifty percent or more of the audience can recall "Winston Tastes Good Like a (bump bump) Cigarette Should," although it has been more than twenty years since the FCC banned that kind of advertising from radio and television! (*Author's Note: Now it's been almost **fifty** years since cigarettes have been legally advertised on electronic media.*) Therefore, the Attitude Control student should read the main text of the book in search of the two, four, six, etc. lines that will most easily replay as a constant reminder to set aside PMA study and meditation time each and every day. You must then write your selected "jingle" at the top of a sheet of paper, and make the commitment to read and reread these rhyming lines, as well as the following exercises on the paper, twice per day, once silently and once aloud for a period of thirty days. Repetition further enhances retention and recall ability. Do this reading early in the day before you begin your normal daily routine; preferably during a quiet time before the distractions come.

2. Go to the front and proceed with reading in a normal progression until you reach the page with the two "trigger" words "BEAUTIFUL" and "FANTASTIC" at the top. At this point, the reader should take pen in hand and decide upon his or her trigger word

or words. Write these beneath the selected "jingle," and follow those with a list (of whatever length) of your blessings—things or life conditions that were nothing but dreams, wishes, or wants ten, five, or even one year ago, and that you have likely been taking for granted lately. The list could be simply the basic conditions that you find necessary to being happy or a longer one which the brain, the fastest computer known to man, can review in the wink of an eye when conditioned to do so. The final statement on the paper should be: "I FELT BAD BECAUSE I HAD NO SHOES UNTIL I MET THE MAN WHO HAD NO FEET!" and/or "THERE, BUT FOR THE GRACE OF GOD, GO I!" THIS LIST WILL BE REVIEWED AT LEAST TWICE PER DAY FOR A PERIOD OF THIRTY DAYS, if you follow the program properly. At the top of the paper, under your jingle, write what is commonly known as a positive affirmation. An example would be: "Today I will have a positive impact on all those I come in contact with" or "I am enthusiastic about helping others achieve their goals" or "I am happy and successful." At the bottom of the page under "There, but for the grace of God, go I," add four of the most powerful words in the English language: "This Too Shall Pass." All things are temporary. This exercise should effectively help to cut short the self-pity parties we so often have, and help your mind to focus on the half-full part of your glass rather than the half-empty, and should implant a positive habit thought pattern in your subconscious mind.

3. The section entitled "OBJECTIFIED WILL" has, after the first two paragraphs, a warning about which I am dead serious. I have found that Self-Help psychology actually has a negative effect when the reader has no defined goals. Therefore, it is necessary at this time to pay attention to an old adage that goes: "A Goal Is Not a Goal Until It Is Written Down!" Therefore, take that same piece of paper, turn it over, and list dreams, wishes, wants, needs, i.e.—goals. Ideally, one or more of these will be a burning goal you have wanted to achieve for some time. Without this special attention to goals, you will not find important the discussion of the human relations revolution directed to entrepreneurs, managers, and supervisors. Nor will you see anything but fanaticism in the section "TO THE INDIVIDUAL," which is designed to help motivate

people in all life stations to excel at their chosen objectives. It is this sense of achievement for managers, laborers, students, professionals, home managers, etc., that can create the euphoria generated when, as Ralph Waldo Emerson in his essay titled "Self Reliance" so eloquently stated, *"A man (woman) is relieved and gay when he (she) has put his (her) heart into his (her) work and done his (her) best; but anything else he (she) says or does shall give him (her) no peace!"*

Goal setting is not a simple task, and I realize that this exercise may require a hiatus of some days or even weeks until your goals have been defined. However, it is an exercise that must be completed before proceeding with the Attitude Control System and with the Objectified Will dissertation.

4. Finally, the "Selected Attitude Control Projects" section should begin (AND CONTINUE FOR LIFE) with the most important book ever written to help one achieve one's goals in life, whatever they may be–the Holy Bible. Since my goal is not to change anyone's religious convictions, my admonition is for you to read the Bible with a somewhat different mindset. Read looking simply for inspiration from those people who persisted toward their goals in spite of the threat of death. Actively look for statements—guidance statements—that can help you achieve any goal you may have: be it health, wealth, companionship or happiness. The books of Acts and Proverbs are literally filled with success instructions and principles.

Lastly, go to the top of the book list and acquire a copy of *The Greatest Salesman in the World* by Og Mandino. Then read and DO the book. It is not necessarily about or for salespeople. It is for all people who desire success, financial independence, self-reliance, greater happiness, etc., etc. It worked for me in spite of the fact that I did it as I was instructed all the while with a skeptical mind. This project will require ten months to complete. Therefore, the "Grunch..."exercises will require approximately one month, and "The Greatest Salesman…" ten months, for a total habit-creating program of eleven months.

Once you have completed "The Greatest Salesman..," go to any of the others on the list, or some other book that you have found in the Self-Help/Inspirational psychology section of your favorite bookstore or library. Control the "Good," positive flow of information that goes into your mind so that good and positive thoughts emerge. Good thoughts attract good things. It works! Try it: you'll like it!

ATTITUDE CONTROL, VERBAL MOOD ELEVATORS, TRIGGER WORDS THAT FOCUS THE MIND ON THE BLESSINGS IN YOUR LIFE WILL WORK TO MAKE LIFE BETTER FOR YOU AND FOR THOSE AROUND YOU!

POSITIVELY,

BOTTOM LINE

"ATTITUDE CONTROL"

A MOTIVATIONAL TRAINING COURSE FOR:
AIDING IN THE ACHIEVEMENT OF GOALS &
IMPROVING THE QUALITY, JOY, FUN, LAUGHTER,
AND, <u>LORD WILLING</u>,
QUANTITY OF YOUR PROFESSIONAL AND PERSONAL LIFE

INTRODUCTION AND/OR
PREFACE, PRELUDE, BEGINNING, COMMENTARY…

It was 1985, and I was driving south on I-75 toward the "50,000-Watt Voice of the Cincinnati Reds" radio station, WLW, when the voice of my old friend "Ralphie," as in Ralph Waldo Emerson, spoke loud and clear: "Show me a man who was saved from nothing, and I'll show you a man who wasn't saved."

I was concerned about how I might convince people that what I call "Attitude Control" really works. While it may not be effective for everyone, it definitely won't be for those who don't give it a try. Those who have put forth the effort have seen their lives enriched in both tangible and intangible respects.

"How," I thought, "can I persuade people in the course of one radio-talk-show appearance about the effectiveness of Attitude Control?!"

Then Ralphie said it again: "Show me a man who…"

I then had a little internal battle with myself: ego versus superego; consciousness versus subconscious; right brain versus left brain. "Self," I thought, "tell the radio audience about… Nah, maybe you shouldn't. After all, you've kept it a secret lo these past 14 years. Oh please, Ralphie, don't make me say it … But I need for people to know–to believe—that it really works! … Okay, that does it."

And so I did.

I told how, in 1971, I was diagnosed to be "hypo-manic/manic-depressive." (I learned during the course of that radio talk show that it is now called a "bi-polar disorder.") I was told that

I should hospitalize myself immediately, so that the proper dosage of sodium lithium could be determined and administered. The details of how this illness totally destroyed my personal and business life make for a classic tale that we needn't take time for right now.

My salvation (I came to realize, with the 20/20 vision of hindsight) came thanks to the pestering encouragement of one Tony Freeman, an employee of mine in Dallas, Texas. Tony kept bugging me to get a copy of "The Little White Book": *The Greatest Salesman in the World* by Og Mandino. My last extended bout with total depression lasted almost two years! I truly thought that I would never recover. I was convinced that I would never again be a functional, contributing member of society.

Slowly, miraculously, I climbed out of that massive depression. I began to think clearly, to take meaningful action, and to return to life, emotionally. But an ominous cloud hung over me. I had identified the fact that my mood swings were on two-year cycles: twelve months of normality, and then six months of accelerating brain activity followed by six months of completely dysfunctional depression. During the period of normality, as the months passed—12, 13, 14, etc.—since The Big Depression, I kept awaiting the symptoms of the next mood swing. Soon, it was two years. Then, three, then four, five, six … and no recurrence! In fact, very seldom did I even have blue periods that lasted more than several minutes. Something was powerful enough to overcome the terrible destructive force that had shattered my life on numerous occasions in the past. But what?

Jump to 1980. I had moved to Dayton, Ohio, and had acquired a staff of telemarketers doing service work for clients. I was trying to inspire, motivate, and, in general, help them with their attitude challenges. At a loss for material, I stopped by a bookstore one evening, and discovered the source of the seeds of my own salvation. It was right there in "the Little White Book" that I had lived with for ten months through portions of 1969 and 1970!!!

My admonition to you, should you desire to gain control over your attitude (the way you think and react to the things in life over which you have no control), should you desire to experience a state of happiness and joy during a greater portion of your life, is to approach the very concept of "self-help psychology" with an open mind. Let the thoughts "Why not?" and "What have I got to lose?" enter your mind now.

Because I would not, or could not, open MY mind (for various reasons which I can now explain), it took me 16 years to realize the positive benefits of "Attitude Control." If you but give the following material a chance, I guarantee that it will work for you in much less time than it did for me. After all, you're probably normal!

Every human being has POTENTIAL control over his/her Attitude; and the operative word in that sentence is "POTENTIAL." The question is whether you will make the commitment to turn "Potential" into "REALITY."

The "Attitude Control Program" is designed to help you begin on a course that will guide and reinforce you for the rest of your natural life. I want to say, "Good Luck," but the words of my mentor, Mark Rednick, always come to mind: ***The harder you work, the luckier you get.***

Attitude Control takes hard work. After all, it must offset the 148,000 negative commands programmed into that most powerful of all personal computers, the one that each of you have perched on your shoulders. So, please remember:

> *It takes hard work to make it well,*
> *But if you'll put forth the effort,*
> *Your _____ will sell!*
> *So spread the word, it's almost like magic,*
> *Without the "Pozzies" the results can be tragic!...*
> *And let it be known and understood,*
> *It's all the harder when times are good!*
>
> --From *The Grunch Who Ate the Bottom Line*

"PERHAPS THE GREATEST DISCOVERY OF MY GENERATION IS THE FACT THAT A MAN CAN ALTER HIS LIFE BY ALTERING HIS ATTITUDE OF MIND!"
--William James, approx. 1910
"GOD NEVER CLOSES ONE DOOR WITHOUT OPENING ANOTHER."

HOW DOES "ATTITUDE CONTROL" WORK?

The following manual is nothing more than an analysis of the thought processes that I experienced in the changing of my Attitude. Once I realized the negative consequences of having an Attitude that was out of my control, I decided to *take control.*

Herewith is how it happened. I have interspersed each Step with a short, inspirational quote gleaned from everywhere. I can't set up your AC Program for you, but for those of you reading a color edition, I can give you the "*blue* prints!" (An Answer Key follows this full program instructional manual.)

"**at·ti·tude** [**at**-i-tood, -tyood] *noun* 1. Position, disposition, or manner with regards to a person or thing: 'a menacing attitude.'"

STEP ONE: FIRST YOU MUST REALIZE THAT YOUR ATTITUDE IS THE RESULT OF A LENGTHY _____ PROCESS.

******

"Write it on your heart that every day is the best day in the year."

--Ralph Waldo Emerson

******

STEP TWO: RECOGNIZING ALL THE OTHER THINGS, CONDITIONS, AND PEOPLE THAT ARE _____ _____ OF YOUR ATTITUDE.

******

Develop the strange new mental disorder called "un-acrophobia": *the fear of <u>not being up</u>*!

******

STEP THREE: REALIZE THAT YOUR LEVEL OF _____ IS PRIMARILY A FACTOR OF HOW YOU _____ TOWARDS THE THINGS THAT HAPPEN TO YOU.

******

"Resolve to see the world on the sunny side,
and you have almost won the battle of life at the outset."

--Sir Roger L'Estrange

STEP FOUR: YOU MUST MAKE A _____ DECISION TO EXPERIENCE MORE HAPPINESS THAN YOU CURRENTLY ARE, AND THAT NO PERSON OR THING HAS THE _____ TO DESTROY YOUR HAPPINESS! RESOLVE TO _____ WHAT YOU HAVE WORKED HARD TO ACHIEVE LIKE MOST PEOPLE GUARD THEIR MOST PRIZED POSSESSIONS.

******

"As a man thinketh in his heart, so is he."

******

STEP FIVE: IF YOUR MIND TRULY ACTS LIKE A _____, (GIGO=Garbage In, Garbage Out), AND IF YOUR ATTITUDE IS THE RESULT OF A _____ PROCESS, YOU MUST SET UP A _____ PROGRAM FOR CONTROLLING YOUR REACTION TO CIRCUMSTANCES WHICH ARE ____ __ _____ _____.

******

"Change your thoughts and you change your world."

-- Dr. Norman Vincent Peale

******

STEP SIX: YOU MUST REALIZE THAT A HABIT IS "n. 1. A disposition or tendency, _____ shown, to act in a certain way; 2. Such a disposition acquired by _____ repetition of an act; 3. A particular _____, custom, or usage; 4. A customary practice or use: to act from force of habit; 5. The mental _____ or disposition: habit of mind." **A HABIT IS FORMED AS A RESULT OF A CONDITIONING PROCESS, AND IS _____.**

******

"Peace is not the absence of conflict,

but the ability to cope with it."

******

STEP SEVEN: A HABIT CAN BE FORMED BY _____ PERFORMING ANY ACT FOR A PERIOD OF _____-____ DAYS (I.E. _____ WEEKS)!

104

******

"None of us is responsible for all of the things that happen to us,

but we are responsible for the way we act when they do happen."

******

STEP EIGHT: IN THE PAST, I HAVE ALLOWED MY _____ TO CONTROL MY _____. IN THE FUTURE, I WILL FORCE MY _____ TO CONTROL MY _____.

******

"It's not the load that breaks you down, it's the way you carry it."

******

STEP NINE: RECOGNIZE THE FACT THAT, FOR MOST OF US, OUR EMOTIONS _____IN A SINE-CURVE FASHION,

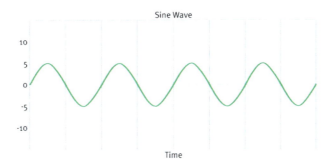

USUALLY AS A RESULT OF CIRCUMSTANCES OUT OF OUR _____. THEREFORE, OUR ACTIVITY LEVEL, WHICH AFFECTS THE _____ ASPECT OF OUR WORK LIVES AND, ULTIMATELY, THE OVERALL _____ OF EVERY ASPECT OF OUR LIVES, MOVES UP AND DOWN PARALLEL TO OUR EMOTIONS CURVE.

MY FRIEND RALPH WALDO EMERSON SAID, "DO YOUR _____ AND I SHALL KNOW YOU. DO YOUR _____ AND YOU SHALL REINFORCE YOURSELF." HE WROTE, "WHAT I MUST DO IS ALL THAT CONCERNS ME. NOT WHAT THE PEOPLE THINK." EVEN THE BIBLE MAKES REFERENCE TO THE IMPORTANCE OF CONSTRUCTIVE ACTIVITY (LABOR) AS A

FACTOR OF HAPPINESS: "WHATEVER THY HAND FINDETH TO DO, DO IT WITH ALL THY MIGHT."

******

"Cheerfulness is contagious. But don't wait to catch it from others. Be a carrier."

******

STEP TEN: RECOGNIZE THE FACT THAT _____, SPECIFICALLY THE OPERATIVE _____ IN A SENTENCE—ESPECIALLY SPOKEN OPERATIVE _____—HAVE, LIKE GEMS, *FACETS*. AN OPERATIVE WORD HAS THREE FACETS:

1. IT HAS ITS HARD, OR CORE, _____.
2. IT HAS THE ABILITY TO EVOKE A MENTAL _____/_____.
3. IT HAS THE ABILITY TO PROVOKE A _____/_____.

IT IS NOW POSSIBLE TO PROVE, MEDICALLY AND SCIENTIFICALLY, THAT THERE CAN BE A PHYSIOLOGICAL REACTION WITHIN OURSELVES AND OTHERS TO WRITTEN AND SPOKEN _____, THROUGH THE STUDY OF BEHAVIORAL KINESIOLOGY!

******

"The plain fact is that human beings are happy only
when they are striving for something worthwhile."

******

STEP ELEVEN: DUE TO THE FACT THAT _____ IS CALLED THE COMMON COLD OF PSYCHIATRY—THEREFORE HAS NO CURE—WE MUST, IN FACT, BUILD UP OUR IMMUNE SYSTEM IN ORDER TO PREVENT IT. BECAUSE THE CAUSE OF _____ MAY BE DUE TO THE CONSTANT INPUT OF NEGATIVE DATA, ONE OF THE FUNDAMENTAL PURPOSES OF "ATTITUDE CONTROL" IS TO PUT IN PLACE A SYSTEM OF "_____-____-_____" AND "BRING-ME-DOWNS." I CALL THESE "MOOD STABILIZERS."

WHEN YOU HAVE PROGRAMMED YOUR MIND PROPERLY, YOU WILL AUTOMATICALLY PRACTICE WHAT I CALL THE "ART OF THOUGHT REPLACEMENT."

******

"A man is rich according to what he is,

not according to what he has."

******

STEP TWELVE: TURN TO YOUR PERSONAL "ATTITUDE CONTROL PAGE," AND BRING A MARKING STICK OF SOME KIND.

******

"A sense of humor can help you overlook the unattractive, tolerate the unpleasant,

cope with the unexpected, and smile through the unbearable."

******

STEP THIRTEEN: IN THIS COPY OF *THE GRUNCH WHO ATE THE BOTTOM LINE!*, SELECT YOUR MOST APPLICALBE, POIGNANT TWO-, FOUR-, OR SIX-LINE "_____" AND REPRODUCE IT IN YOUR OWN _____ AT THE TOP OF THE PAGE. SHOULD YOU BE UNABLE TO FIND ONE THAT FITS, THEN CREATE YOUR OWN. WHY?

******

"Yesterday's failures and tomorrow's worries leave little room for today's blessings."

******

STEP FOURTEEN: DECIDE UPON AND WRITE YOUR "_____ WORDS" UNDER THE SELECTED JINGLE.

******

"When a man finds no peace within himself, it is useless to seek it elsewhere."

******

STEP FIFTEEN: LIST ALL OF THE _____ YOU NOW ENJOY, OR JUST THOSE YOU HAVE DECIDED YOU BASICALLY NEED TO BE HAPPY, AND LAUNCH YOURSELF TO FAME AND FORTUNE. _____ CAN

BE DREAMS NOW REALIZED OR SIMPLY THINGS, MATERIAL OR IMMATERIAL, THAT YOU AT ONE TIME HAD TO DO WITHOUT. THE CONSCIOUS MIND WORKS MUCH MORE _____ THAN THE SUBCONSCIOUS. THEREFORE, THE LIST OF BLESSINGS CAN BE AS LENGTHY AS YOU WANT AND, ONCE SET IN MOTION, CAN REVIEW ANY NUMBER OF ITEMS IN A SPLIT NANOSECOND!

******

"It is almost impossible to smile on the outside without feeling better on the inside."

******

STEP SIXTEEN: AT THE BOTTOM OF THIS PAGE, WRITE THE EXPRESSION(S): "I FELT BAD BECAUSE I HAD NO _____, UNTIL I MET THE MAN WHO HAD NO _____," AND/OR "THERE, BUT FOR THE GRACE OF _____, GO I!" AND FOUR WORDS I WILL TRAIN MYSELF TO SAY: "_____ _____ _____ _____."

HOW TRUE THIS IS FOR ALL OF US LUCKY ENOUGH TO BE LIVING IN THIS GREAT COUNTRY! EVEN IN THE WORST POSSIBLE SCENARIO, THERE ARE THOSE WHO ARE WORSE OFF THAN WE.

I CALL THE WORDS YOU HAVE WRITTEN ON THIS PAGE "VERBAL MOOD _____." I HAVE OFTEN SAID, "THE MOST EFFECTIVE (OR CRUEL) THING ONE PERSON CAN DO TO ANOTHER IS TO USE HIS/HER OWN _____ ON HIM/HER!" WELL, NOW YOU MUST USE YOUR OWN ON YOURSELF.

******

"Some people succeed because they are destined to,
but most people succeed because they are determined to."

******

STEP SEVENTEEN: TURN YOUR "A.C." PAGE OVER.

******

"The first thought in the morning and the last thought at night
are marked on your face and the set of your shoulders."

******

STEP EIGHTEEN: DRAW TWO STRAIGHT LINES WHICH INTERSECT AT RIGHT ANGLES IN THE CENTER OF THE PAGE. MARK THE SECTION FORMED IN THE UPPER LEFT CORNER #1, THE UPPER RIGHT, #2, THE LOWER LEFT, #3, AND THE LOWER RIGHT, #4.

PER THE EXAMPLE THAT FOLLOWS THIS PROGRAM, SQUARE #1 IS FOR YOU TO LIST YOUR _____ AND _____. SQUARE #2 IS FOR YOUR _____. #3 IS FOR YOUR _____, AND #4 FOR YOUR _____ IN _____ ORDER (I.E. IN ORDER OF THAT WHICH YOU BELIEVE YOU CAN ACCOMPLISH FIRST, SECOND, THIRD, ETC., GIVEN YOUR PRESENT CIRCUMSTANCES).

REMEMBER: A GOAL IS NOT A GOAL UNTIL IT'S _____ DOWN! AND THINK ABOUT THE OLD ADAGE: "SHOUT YOUR GOALS TO THE WORLD AND YOU HAVE NO ALTERNATIVE BUT TO SUCCEED."

******

"Let us train our minds to desire what the situation demands."

******

STEP NINETEEN: SUGGESTED THOUGHTS TO READ ALOUD NOW:

"WHAT DO I HAVE TO LOSE? JUST IN CASE IT MIGHT WORK TO MAKE MY LIFE HEALTHIER, WEALTHIER, AND HAPPIER, I WILL MAKE A 30-DAY COMMITMENT. I WILL ARISE EACH MORNING AND READ WHAT I HAVE WRITTEN ONCE SILENTLY, AND AGAIN, BEFORE I BEGIN THE DISTRACTING, FRUSTRATING, CHALLENGING ACTIVITIES OF THE DAY AHEAD, READ THEM ALOUD.

"I KNOW IT TAKES SIX SPACED REPETITIONS OF ANYTING FOR MY MIND TO RETAIN AND HAVE TOTAL RECALL OF 95% OF ANY INFORMATION FOR THE REST OF MY LIFE! 60 REPETITIONS FROM NOW, I WILL BE READY FOR OG MANDINO'S 10-MONTH CHALLENGE! I'LL TRY IT AND, IF IT WORKS FOR ME, I'LL SHARE IT WITH OTHERS."

******

"Nobody ever finds life worth living,

One always has to make it worth living."

******

PERSISTENCE IS THE KEY

ATTITUDE CONTROL IS THE WAY TO THE KEY

WISHES/DREAMS   WANTS

1.   1.

2.   2.

3.   3.

NEEDS   NEEDS PRIORITIZED

1.   1.

2.   2.

3.   3.

MY FIRST "ATTITUDE CONTROL" PROGRAM

JINGLE:

_____

_____

_____

_____

TRIGGER WORDS:

➤ _____

➤ _____

➤ _____

➤ _____

➤ _____

POSITIVE AFFIRMATIONS:

_____

_____

_____

BLESSINGS THAT MAKE MY GLASS HALF FULL:

1. _____

2. _____

3. _____

ANTI   SELF-PITY   THOUGHT(S): _____

_____

_____

WISHES/DREAMS

1. _____
2. _____
3. _____
4. _____
5. _____

WANTS

1. _____
2. _____
3. _____
4. _____
5. _____

NEEDS

1. _____
2. _____
3. _____
4. _____
5. _____

NEEDS PRIORITIZED

1. _____
2. _____
3. _____
4. _____
5. _____

KEY FOR ATTITUDE CONTROL PROGRAMMED INSTRUCTION

1. conditioning
2. in control
3. happiness, react
4. conscious, right, protect
5. computer, conditioning, consistent, out of your control
6. constantly, frequent, practice, character, powerful
7. consistently, twenty-one, three
8. emotions, actions, actions, emotions
9. fluctuate, control, happiness, happiness, happiness, thing, work
10. words, words, words, meaning, picture/image, feeling/emotion, words
11. depression, depression, pick-me-ups
12. N/A
13. jingle, handwriting
14. trigger
15. blessings, blessings, quickly
16. shoes, feet, God, elevators, words, This Too Shall Pass
17. N/A
18. wishes, dreams, wants, needs, needs, priority
19. written

ON HUMOR & LAUGHTER

"Life is far too important to be taken seriously." – Oscar Wilde

I use the quote above as the heading of many of my email messages. I use silly props at my speeches and seminars in large part because of several quotes from "The Scroll Marked VII" in Og Mandino's *The Greatest Salesman in the World* (most of all, I encourage everyone to incorporate the last quote in the following list into your personality, character, and every aspect of your attitude):

"I will laugh at the world."

"No living creature can laugh except man."

"…Henceforth I will cultivate the habit of laughter."

"I will smile and my digestion will improve; I will chuckle and my burdens will be lightened; I will laugh and my life will be lengthened for this is the great secret of long life and now it is mine."

"I will laugh at the world."

"And most of all I will laugh at myself, for man is most comical when he takes himself too seriously."

Not too many years ago I could never have worn an outsized pseudo-safety pin that appears to be going through my head, a huge squeakable pseudo-baby pacifier strung around my neck, nor an outsized pair of yellow sunglasses. Of course, each has a special message, but most of all I can "make a fool of myself" and realize that I once was most "comical when I took myself too seriously". Could it be that my audience, my seminar/training attendees, laugh due to the juxtaposition of silliness against my formal business attire of suit and tie?

Some years ago I heard Zig Ziglar say that research at the Ziglar Corporation in Dallas, Texas, had shown that the attention span of an audience is enhanced by 300 to 1000% if something humorous happens every six to eight minutes. I then saw an article in the *USA Today* newspaper that avowed that school children have an innate attention span of no more than FIVE MINUTES! Of course, I contend that we, as adults, have an even shorter attention span since we have so many responsibilities, obligations, errands, thoughts, plans, and happenings to distract our focus. So is it any wonder that one could almost set a clock when attending a presentation by Zig. He almost

114

never failed to interject something that had the entire room laughing in the six to eight minute time frame.

Ask yourself, how often have you been watching a movie or some sitcom on TV, or even a stand-up comedian, and, when everyone else in the room began laughing, you found that you had allowed your wandering mind to miss the punch line. You nudged the person next to you and asked "What was said? What did I miss?" Why? Because it feels good to laugh. It not only feels good, it has been proven that laughter, hearty belly-roll laughter releases endorphins and serotonin and increases the flow of T-Cells in the blood stream to help prevent and/or cure disease. Laughter has been proven to aid in the cure rate of patients. I cannot recommend enough the book by Norman Cousins *Anatomy Of An Illness as Perceived by the Patient (How One Man Proved Your Mind Can Cure Your Body).*

I find it interesting that, early on in the history of the practice of medicine, the body was thought to contain four "humors," also spelled humours:

"The four humors of Hippocratic medicine are black bile (Gk. Melan, chole), yellow bile (Gk. Chole), phlegm (Gk. Phlegm), and blood (Gk. Haima), and each corresponds to one of the traditional four temperaments.

"Four temperaments is a proto-psychological interpretation of the ancient medical concept of humorism and suggests that four bodily fluids affect human personality traits and behaviors. The temperaments are sanguine (pleasure-seeking and sociable), choleric (ambitious and leader-like), melancholic (introverted and thoughtful), and phlegmatic (relaxed and quiet).

"The Greek physician Hippocrates (460-370 BC) incorporated the four temperaments into his medical theories. From then through modern times, they, or modifications of them, have been a part of many theories of medicine, psychology and literature."

-- ***Wikipedia,*** The Four Humors

Hmmm ... so the four "humors" and the four "temperaments" are related? And a sense of humor and laughter relate to a person's personality. Verrry intellesting.

My mentor Mark Rednick, who could literally tell 5,000 jokes back to back without repetition, used to say, "jokes are all based on someone else's pain, pratfall, embarrassment, ethnicity, heritage and are quite negative when you think about them". Humor is different in that, like what Bill Cosby and Robin Williams and Dave Barry and Mark Twain did, humorists stretch and contort real life situations into shapes that make us laugh.

"Humour or humor (see spelling differences) is the tendency of particular cognitive experiences to provoke laughter and provide amusement. The term derives from the humoral medicine of the ancient Greeks, which taught that the balance of fluids in the human body, known as humors (Latin. Humor, "body fluid"), control human health and emotion.

"People of all ages and cultures respond to humour. The majority of people are able to experience humour, i.e., to be amused, to laugh or smile at something funny, and thus they are considered to have a sense of humour. The hypothetical person lacking a sense of humour would likely find the behavior induced by humour to be inexplicable, strange, or even irrational. Though ultimately decided by personal taste, the extent to which a person will find something humourous depends upon a host of variables, including geographical location, culture, maturity, level of education, intelligence and context. For example, young children may favour slapstick, such as Punch and Judy puppet shows or cartoons such as Tom and Jerry. Satire may rely more on understanding the target of the humour and thus tends to appeal to more mature audiences."

-- ***Wikipedia,*** Humor

Due to my desire to add humor to my presentations as well as more humor to my life, I discovered Joel Goodman's Humor Project many years ago. I found it a real eye-opener when one of his quarterly publications, called "Laughing Matters," had in it an audit form. It asked me to analyze what kind of humor and/or funny-ness gave me a real hearty laugh. I had never thought about the different types of humor nor given any thought to which type had the most impact on my funny bone. After some thought I realized it is what is commonly known as "dry humor." Richard Wright does my kind of humor, always funny with a "straight face." Alex Karras, the late actor and former professional football player, has totally cracked me up. The grandson of the founder of psychiatry, Clement Freud, has caused me to virtually fall on the floor laughing. Once my audit was complete, I was encouraged to look for comedians and other opportunities to experience those things that would generate hearty laughter using the kind of material that makes me laugh uproariously. Mr. Goodman also suggested that I keep a journal in which to describe the things that gave me a good laugh so I could refer to them whenever I felt I needed one or two.

There is a new thing called "Laughter Yoga," whereby people simply force laughter due to the fact that it's been determined that good benefits result from either a genuine or a faked laugh. As described by *Wikipedia.*

"Laughter Yoga (*Hasyayoga*) is a form of yoga employing self-triggered laughter. The concept of Laughter Yoga is based on the scientific observation that the body cannot differentiate between fake and real laughter, and that both provide the same physiological and psychological benefits. Laughter Yoga combines unconditional laughter with pranayama (yogic breathing). Laughter is simulated as a body exercise in a group; with eye contact and childlike playfulness, initially forced laughter soon turns into real and contagious laughter. The "laughter" is physical in nature, and does not necessarily involve humor or comedy.

"Laughter Yoga was made popular as an exercise routine developed by Indian physician Madan Kataria, who writes about the practice in his book *Laugh For No Reason.*

"In the mid-1990s, Laughter Yoga was practiced in the early mornings, primarily by groups of older men in open parks. Later, a more formalized version was created and popularized as "Laughter Clubs." Kataria's first Laughter Yoga Club began on 13 March 1995 in Mumbai; beginning with five people in a local public park, the concept has rapidly spread worldwide. As of 2011, there are more than 8,000 Laughter Clubs in 65 countries. Each club has its own Laugh Captain and operates as an independent cell.

"Laughter is easily stimulated in a group when combined with eye contact, 'childlike playfulness' and laughter exercises. Fake laughter quickly becomes real. Laughter Yoga brings more oxygen to the body and brain by incorporating yogic breathing which results in deep diaphragmatic breathing.

"Laughter Yoga is a unique exercise routine which combines unconditional laughter with yogic breathing (Pranayama). Anyone can laugh without needing to rely on humor, jokes or comedy. Laughter is initially simulated as a physical exercise while maintaining eye contact with others in the group and promoting childlike playfulness. In most cases this soon leads to real and contagious laughter. Scientific studies have demonstrated that the body does not differentiate between simulated and real laughter. Laughter Yoga is the only technique that allows adults to achieve sustained hearty laughter without involving cognitive thought. It bypasses the intellectual systems that normally act as a brake on natural laughter."

Many years ago I knew a young lady named Peggy. She made me laugh, and had such a constant sense of humor that I actually asked her a question I dislike a lot: "Peggy, are you ever serious?"

She said, "I think people should laugh at least fifty percent of the time."

I said, "Wow! If people aren't laughing while sleeping, then they'd be laughing about two-thirds of the time they're awake."

Peggy said, "So?"

Most women say, the number one thing they want in their men is a "sense of humor". So guys, you'd better get with it. Ladies, I think the same can be said for you.

A sense of humor totally relates to your attitude. Laughter puts life in perspective.

"I will laugh at the world."

TWENTY EIGHT YEARS OF RANDOM—AND POSSIBLY ICONOCLASTIC—THOUGHTS, RUMINATIONS, REGURGITATIONS, QUOTES, PROFUNDITIES & STUFF

So, what have I learned over these past decades? A sweatshirt that a friend gifted me some years ago contains the Italian phrase "Aun Aprendo," which means, "I am still learning." I hope that is still true.

(All of the following topics relate in some way to the general topic of ATTITUDE CONTROL)

Attitude

I have an attitude. You have an attitude. Human nature gave us all an attitude. Now it's up to us to achieve something I call "Attitude Control."

I define attitude as "how we react to the things that happen to us that are outside of our control." With enough thought, it is possible to realize that most of the major things we allow to impact whether we have a positive or negative attitude are, in fact, out of our control. Eleanor Roosevelt stated, "No other person can make us feel inferior without our permission." I contend, "No other thing, person or situation can control our attitude without our permission." Each of us must make the conscious decision to practice the habit of reacting positively toward anything that happens, be it the weather, the world economy, the catching of a cold, the stranger who snubs us, the unexpected flat tire on the car, the stain that appears on our clothing after arriving at work or a special event, etc., etc. Here are two versions of a very familiar quote on the subject of attitude:

"The longer I live; the more I realize the impact of attitude on life. Attitude, to me, is more important than facts. It is more important than the past, than education, than money, than circumstances, than failures, than successes, than what other people think or say or do. It is more important than appearance, giftedness or skill. It will make or break a company…a church…a home. The remarkable thing is, we have a choice every day regarding the attitude we will embrace for that day. We cannot change our past…we cannot change the fact that people will act in a certain way, we cannot change the inevitable. The only thing we can do is play on the one string we have, and that is our attitude. I am convinced that life is 10% what happens to me and 90% how I react to it. And so it is with you … We are in charge of our Attitudes."*

Stated slightly differently:

"Words can never adequately convey the incredible impact of our attitude toward life. The longer I live, the more convinced I become that life is 10% what happens to us and 90% how we respond to it."

I believe the single most significant decision I can make on a day-to-day basis is my choice of attitude. It is more important than my past, my education, my bankroll, my successes or failures, fame or pain, what other people think of me or say about me, my circumstances, or my position. Attitude keeps me going or cripples my progress. It alone fuels my fire or assaults my hope. When my attitudes are right, there's no barrier too high, no valley too deep, no dream too extreme, no challenge too great for me.

It was over two and a half decades ago that we–my new bride, Judy, and I–left Ohio on a national book promotion tour in "The Grunch Mobile," a thirty-four-foot-long motor home towing a little white car. (I was amazed by the number of people who, upon observing our mode of travel and hearing about our adventure, said, "That's my dream–to one day sell my home, buy one of those, and travel to my heart's content." I would think, "This is a free country, so why do you postpone your 'dream'"? What if that "one day" never comes? Then your dream becomes a regret.)

Our tow car contained professionally-made signage: "It's a 'BEAUTIFUL' day!!!" "Make Your Own Sunshine" and "Honk If You're Happy." Our one year of traveling this fantastic country provided experiences for a lifetime, sights one never sees from airplanes–lakes and oceans, eastern and western sunsets (oftentimes different as night and day), hills and mountains and valleys and canyons and arroyos and cacti and green, brown, and magenta on the land, and rainbows and fall yellows, golds, reds and oranges and clouds–oh, the clouds, and shooting stars and trees … and conversations with some of the most interesting people one could hope to meet. (I had told Judy what I had anticipated seeing out our little picture window by the breakfast table during the coming year, and it all came to pass. AND IT WAS BEAUTIFUL!)

And as for those "most interesting people," that would include "L.C.," his two initials that when spoken rapidly are heard as "Elsie"! He was a tall, elegant African-American waiter at Marie

120

LeVeau's restaurant in the French Quarter of New Orleans. There were Kenneth and Marianne Jones of Natchez, Mississippi, whom we happened upon at a scenic rest area in New England. There was Kevin from Buffalo, New York; Wayne Soule in Phoenix; Norma in the Glen Iris Inn at Letchworth State Park in the Finger Lakes region of western New York State.

All of these people–and many more–were subjected to three questions:

1. What do you want to be when you grow up?

2. If you had the power to go back in your life and change or do one thing differently, what would that one thing be?

3. If I were your favorite person and you had one last chance to give me a piece of advice that would hold me in good stead through the remainder of my life, what would that advice be?

The answers are preserved on some "floppy discs" located–carefully stored (aw, what the heck, they're piled helter skelter) somewhere in the garage…I think. The profound ones have been oft repeated, and are on the tip of my tongue to share with whomever will listen.

On Question #1:

The older the person, the more interesting, humorous, entertaining, and profound the response. "A fireman." "A policeman." Sadly, some said, "I'm already grown up." L.C. said, "A professional bike-rider." Although the question seems open-ended and truly subjective, I was looking for the "right" answer. "Except as ye become as little children, ye shall not enter the kingdom of heaven." Seems to me the "right" answer is: "I refuse to grow up." (I've come to the conclusion one can be "child-like" without being "childish; and one can act in a mature fashion when the occasion calls for it and then return to being child-like.)

After all, children wonder about things–how grass grows, trees, sunsets, clouds, spider webs, dirt. To them, the world is full of wonder; or should I say "wonder-full." Somehow, some way, growing up precludes some of that wonder-fullness for adults in this world. Time flies when one quits wondering. Slowing time means living in the present. Yoga and the very act of meditation emphasize the concept of capturing awareness of the present. Kids come by it quite naturally.

On Question #2:

By its very nature, this question is egocentric. For most people, the personal pronoun "I" captures their thinking; therefore most people responded with such things as, "I would have gone to college" or "I wouldn't have married so young the first time" or "I…" But it was eighty-one-year young Norma, the guest of honor in a group celebrating her birthday one day at lunch in the Glen Iris Inn at Letchworth State Park, New York, who provided the most profound, and now what I consider to be the "right," response: "I would have made people love each other more." This she said as I knelt by her with my hand lying softly on her forearm. I was taken aback by the fact that she had thought, FIRST AND FOREMOST, not of herself and what she would alter in her personal history, but of others. For quite some time I had thought that the "right" response would be, "Nothing, for, being happy with who I am today, I wouldn't change a thing". Because of Norma, I have changed my conviction about the "rightest" answer to this question.

(Due to the large number of people helping Norma celebrate her birthday at noon on a weekday, I said, "Norma, because you appear to think of other people first, is it safe to assume that you have a lot of friends?" With a twinkle in her eyes, she responded, "They say I do.")

(Oh yeah, and L.C. said in answer to Question #2: "I'd a bin a better gambler". I wonder if he's now playing Texas Hold'em somewhere, or if he swore off gambling for life???)

On Question #3:

This one got all kinds of unique responses. But the table of elderly gentlemen in a restaurant in the Berkshires of upstate New York, all of whom appeared to be at least septuagenarians, took the cake. The five occupants of that table represented in excess of 350 years of life's experiences, so I couldn't resist. My wife had departed our table for the "powder room" when I approached that table of potential wisdom and interrupted their meal, deciding that Question #3 would be the only one I'd likely be permitted the time to get responses from each of them. White-haired Number One said "Be honest." I commented that, "My grandfather would have liked that, since his philosophy was 'I care not a man's religion, color or country of origin, I care only that he be honest'". Elderly gentleman Number Three dittoed the advice of Number Two who said, "Enjoy your work". Number Four started the laughter with, "Save your money and buy good whiskey." But it was the very last wise guy who advised, "Keep your head cool, your feet

122

warm, and your bowels open." I had thought he was making light of the fact that the older we get, the more important the topic of "regularity" becomes. But, no.

I was feverishly writing their responses on a napkin when Judy returned to our table and asked several times what I was doing. I couldn't respond until I had returned to the featured table and asked for a repeat of the last fellow's response, so I could make sure I had it right. After completing my transcription, I revealed to Judy what I had learned. We laughed together and then…some years later I noticed how often I heard that someone had passed away due to a "bowel obstruction." I'll never know how serious that temporary mentor had been with his response to my question; nevertheless, it appears to be very good advice, and I've learned that a proper diet and exercise can facilitate making "open bowels" a fact of life.

But what does all this have to do with the primary thrust of this book and "Attitude Control"? Don't worry, it's all relative.

On The Education Myth

I, as a former teacher, as well as those teachers I had during my formal education, promised students that the world would be their oyster if they simply put forth the effort to get one of those sheepskins from an institution of higher learning. Then I learned that many of the world's most successful and wealthiest business people had/have a limited formal education! Bill Gates dropped out of Harvard. Michael Dell did likewise. J. Paul Getty, Andrew Carnegie, and, more recently the 9th, 10th, 11th, 14th, and 17th wealthiest people in the world, who have no more than a high school education, obviously also eschewed formal education and yet realized great economic success. (However, please be aware of the fact that I am not equating the achievement of wealth with the generic meaning of the word "success." I also believe that one should be "rich" prior to becoming "wealthy," for there is a difference. I encourage everyone to become aware of that very significance difference.)

I am most disappointed with the fact that our institutions of higher learning, i.e., colleges and universities, have effectively become nothing more than expensive "vocational schools" that churn out workers for today's industries rather than educate human beings who can think with clarity and logic. Want a job? Go to college. Want an education? Go to…? Google? Wikipedia? World

Wide Web? KahnAcademy.org? Coursera? Udacity? Associate with smart people who can arouse your curiosity about everything.

I have long thought that one of my heroes, Ralph Waldo Emerson, would be terribly disenchanted with today's colleges and universities. Early on, all institutions of higher learning provided what can only be called liberal arts degrees. Many were founded with religious or church affiliations. You were confined to the study of theology, history, literature, philosophy, etc.–the humanities, they're called today. To major in the humanities is to forego getting a good, high-paying job, but just maybe an education.

On The Self-Employment Failure Myth

"For non-conformity the world whips you with it displeasure."
--Ralph Waldo Emerson

To conform means to get a job. Non-conformity means, doing your own thing and becoming self-employed. But, alas! Be afraid! Eighty percent, four out of five, small businesses will not exist within five years of start-up. That statistic should be enough to guarantee that no fool with an ounce of common sense should ever leave the security of working for someone else. Sadly enough, another statistic makes a mockery of the former statement: "Most economically successful people have been involved in as many as five or six or more other ventures prior to initiating the one that resulted in their fortunes."

I, personally, have been involved in numerous start-ups. Several have failed and disappeared. Several I sold, and the new owner changed the business name; thus, to the statisticians there was a vendor's license or an employer ID that disappeared from the rolls–both of which indicated to the uninformed that a person had failed. Not true. A person committed to being the "Captain of his fate, The master of his soul" continued on to the next venture.

One of my favorite sayings is inscribed on a plaque on the wall of my office: "You're never a failure until you quit trying."

Entrepreneurism is risky; self-employment, not necessarily (or "…not so much."). Entrepreneurism means breaking new ground, inventing or creating something new to the universe. Self-employment can mean doing something as old as the hills, like carpentry or food service or prostitution, and being in control of doing it. So, how can one become self-employed without experiencing a high degree of risk? Franchising is just one method. Then there are existing, successful businesses to purchase. There are existing successful business concepts that can be transplanted to a market big enough to support them. There are people who love their freedom to devote a random day or hour to their families or their avocation or to nothing at all WITHOUT GETTING PERMISSION FROM A BOSS–BUT WHO ARE ALSO WILLING TO PERSIST UNTIL THEY SUCCEED. Methinks those of us who have the entrepreneurial/self-employment spirit are rebels at heart or, at the least, don't kowtow to "authority figures". Methinks that most of those who innovate, who plow that "new ground" and who illuminate new vistas, were imbued with similar characters. I know that, on many occasions, I've been called a "character" and a rebel.

Is it possible that some successful entrepreneurs are created as a result of the conclusion of Robert Heinlein: "Progress isn't made by early risers. It's made by lazy men trying to find easier ways to so something." Food for thought, eh?

"Times, fads, fashions and people change, but principles never." Og Mandino wrote that in his inspired book, The Greatest Salesman In The World. What worked 2000 years ago will work as well today–if it is based upon a principle–a valid MORAL principle.

Could it be that the only thing one has to fear about self-employment is "fear itself?" Could it be a conspiracy to keep people working for other people? After all, wasn't there a time in human history when almost all productivity was generated by what were called "cottage industries"? These were small businesses such as farms, coopers, blacksmiths, seamstresses, working on their plot of ground or from their homes or small shops located in close proximity.

"Nothing ventured, nothing gained." After interviewing quite a number of people who had been terminated from their jobs at an advanced age when it would be much more difficult to find another, I determined that, if I was going to have to adjust to the challenges of starting a business and the financial insecurity that often accompanies such an endeavor, I wanted to make the necessary adjustments as a younger man when resiliency and temporary failure doesn't appear to be fatal. This does not mean that one cannot be a successful entrepreneur at an advanced age. (Check out the story of Colonel Harlan Sanders of Kentucky Fried Chicken fame.) Necessity can truly be the mother of invention and of a successful small business enterprise. So, go for it, and when you face that fork in the road, take the one your heart moves you to choose. Once again, if it's something you have a passion for and that you know you will enjoy doing, then remember the words of one of my boyhood baseball idols, Cleveland Indians pitcher and Hall of Famer Bob Feller, who said: "If you can find something to do for a living that you enjoy, you'll never work a day in your life."

If I've written this already in one of these essays, it still bears repeating:

In the words of my former employer and mentor, Mark Rednick, as I resigned my job to enter the world of self-employment: "Make me one promise…that you'll always let money be a fringe benefit of all the fun you're having. Think about it. If you're having fun, you'll do it well. If you do it well, the money will take care of itself."

I've added one thing to that admonition: "…fun AND DOING GOOD FOR OTHER PEOPLE, the money will take care of itself." It dovetails rather nicely with old Zig's "You can have everything you want in life if you help enough other people get what they want."

"Do your thing and I shall know you; do your work and you shall reinforce yourself." Above all, DO YOUR THING. Only then can you truly be "The Captain of your fate; the master of your soul."

Employee-owned businesses are offering many of the incentives and benefits of self-employment. Some companies, such as Cleveland, Ohio-based Lincoln Electric, have created compensation plans that engender an "ownership attitude." That attitude causes people to work more dependably, efficiently, and productively, as well as to care about the cost factors relative to their job functions and to the company as a whole.

The Dana Corporation, one of the companies featured in Tom Peters' and Robert H. Waterman's *In Search of Excellence*, does something quite unique to help engender a sense of ownership among its factory workers. While I have looked high and low for the actual quote regarding the Dana Corporation (now known as the Dana Holding Company), I find it necessary to do my best at paraphrasing what I recall reading:

A Dana plant manager gathers all of the several hundreds of production employees into one area of the plant and, his/her voice amplified by a megaphone, shares the production and quality–with an emphasis on waste–numbers with the entire workforce.

This simple act, which I'm quite sure does not require a great deal of paid time commitment on the part of management, informs the first-line workers so they can take ownership in the kind of quality performance that affects productivity and profitability. It means they have some control over keeping their jobs. Far too often, management keeps hidden the numbers that might indicate the amount of profit the business is making–as though that fact might cause rebellion amongst the troops. This might be true if that profitability is outrageous, and too much goes to the top and stockholders rather than being fairly shared throughout the workforce or reinvested in the company. But as Dr. Deming pointed out, "it's the first-line workers who know best how to improve productivity, efficiency and quality–so solicit suggestions from them, and then listen and incorporate the valid ones."

Far too often, companies keep their people in the dark when it comes to the numbers, thus allowing their imaginations to rule over rational decision-making when it comes to their perceived "fair wage."

Most importantly, I want Attitude Control to be as applicable to every member of an organization and team–because everyone is critical to the success of the whole.

*Charles Swindoll. STRENGTHENING YOUR GRIP. (Nashville: W. Publishing Group, 1982), pp. 206-7. Used by permission of Insight for Living, Plano, TX 75026

Grunch **Self-employment Disclaimer:** Although this essay is meant to dispel the fears associated with attempting self-employment, I want to assure the reader that I hope I am not appearing to downplay the essential nature of everyone who contributes to the success of all business ventures. My "lovely bride" often accuses me of being pedantic when it comes to my attitude toward those who "work for a boss." In no way is that my purpose, for there are many justifiable reasons why people may choose a career with less risk, less stress and a guaranteed income with benefits and the synergy of working with a team. In fact, one of my primary goals is to encourage and present methods and promote attitudes that can help everyone experience joy and satisfaction from whatever career path that they choose, and however they earn a living.

Marsha Sinetar's "Do What You Love, The Money Will Follow," subtitled "Finding Your Right Livelihood," extols the virtues of generating an income by identifying what one's passion is and then finding employment–or self-employment–that incorporates that passion. I have long stated that "life is too short to dread Mondays, live for Fridays and weekends, and think of Wednesdays as "hump day." To enjoy life ONLY on weekends is to live a maximum of one-hundred four days per year!

Don't let that happen to you.

I repeat the words of the Hall of Fame baseball pitcher Bob Feller: "If you can find something to do for a living that you enjoy, you'll never work a day in your life." Whether that's doing your own thing in the world of self-employment, or generating an income working for someone else or for an organization, it matters not. Life should be a joy ride, and since we devote a majority of our lives to our careers it–whatever you choose–should be enjoyable and joyful.

128

WHY I PICK UP HIKERS & HITCHHIKERS (AND THE OCCASIONAL CYCLER): AVOIDING A BIT OF HUMANITY'S HYPOCRISY

My tennis buddy, John Lantz, was overheard saying "Hey, he picks up hitchhikers, too." (He failed to mention that I also pick up hikers if they appear to need something I can provide.) It's a small skirmish in my battle with that human frailty called hypocrisy.

You see, at one time in my life, I did a good bit of hitchhiking. So how can I not do for others what others did for me? How many times did I find myself standing alongside a highway, hand out with my thumb pointing skyward and repeating in my mind, "Oh, c'mon, you have five empty seats, and all that empty space is moving in the direction I need to go. Please, please pick me up. I'm not dangerous. I just want to get where I'm going. I'll help make your ride go faster by conversing on any topic you wish. Please. I'm cold, hot, wet, tired, hungry, miserable. Please pick me up."

So, what John said was meant to emphasize the fact that I am "different." I wear my "differentness" as a badge of honor. I hope it confirms that I "march to the beat of a different drummer," that I live a bit according to those fabulous words of Emerson, who said in his essay "Self Reliance": "A foolish consistency is the hobgoblin of little minds, adored by little statesmen and philosophers and divines. With consistency, a great mind has simply nothing to do." Below are just a few of the other powerful quotes from "Self Reliance":

"…To believe your own thought, to believe that what is true for you in your private heart is true for all men—that is genius."

"…Society everywhere is in conspiracy against the manhood of every one of its members. Society is a joint-stock company, in which the members agree, for the better securing of his bread to each shareholder, to surrender the liberty and culture of the eater. The virtue in most request is conformity. Self-reliance is its aversion. It loves not realities and creators, but names and customs."

"Whoso would be a man must be a nonconformist."

"What I must do is all that concerns me, not what the people think. This rule, equally arduous in actual and in intellectual life, may serve for the whole distinction between greatness and meanness. It is the harder, because you will always find those who think they know what your duty is better than you know it. It is easy in the world to live after the world's opinion; it is easy in solitude to live after our own; but the great man is he who in the midst of the crowd keeps with perfect sweetness the independence of solitude."

"For nonconformity the world whips you with its displeasure."

"A foolish consistency is the hobgoblin of little minds, adored by little statesmen and philosophers and divines. With consistency a great soul has simply nothing to do. He may as well concern himself with his shadow on the wall. Speak what you think now in hard words, and to-morrow speak what to-morrow thinks in hard words again, though it contradict everything you said to-day.—'Ah, so you shall be sure to be misunderstood.'—Is it so bad, then, to be misunderstood? Pythagoras was misunderstood, and Socrates, and Jesus, and Luther, and Copernicus, and Galileo, and Newton, and every pure and wise spirit that ever took flesh. To be great is to be misunderstood."

"I hope in these days we have heard the last of conformity and consistency."

"It is easy to see that a greater self-reliance must work a revolution in all the offices and relations of men; in their religion; in their education; in their pursuits; their modes of living; their association; in their property; in their speculative views."

But back to the core of this essay: hiking and hitchhiking. Without my penchant for paying forward the kindness of others when I was in need of a ride, I would never have met Dr. John Francis, aka The Planet Walker, or Elijah Alexander, Jr., aka "Nature Boy." You can Google them and learn why I consider that just meeting and getting to know the two of them has made my non-conformity a totally worthwhile endeavor.

At the very least, I need to share one more powerful quote, and this one from Elbert Hubbard's scrapbook. I hope it will inspire more people to "take a hike":

"I do not think that I exaggerate the importance or the charms of pedestrianism, or our need as a people to cultivate the art. I think it would tend to soften the national manners, to teach us the meaning of leisure, to acquaint us with the charms of the open air, to strengthen and foster the tie between the race and the land. No one else looks out upon the world so kindly and charitably as does the pedestrian; no one gives and takes so much from the country he passes through. Next to the laborer in the fields, the walker holds the closest relation to the soil; and he holds a closer and more vital relation to Nature because he is freer and is more at leisure.

"Man takes root at his feet, and at best he is no more than a potted plant in his house or carriage till he has established communication with the soil by the loving and magnetic touch of his soles to it. Then the tie of association is born; then those invisible fibers and rootlets through which character comes to smack of the soil, and which makes a man kindred to the spot of earth he inhabits.

"The roads and paths you have walked along in Summer and Winter weather, the meadows and hills which you have looked upon in lightness and gladness of heart, where fresh thought have come into your mind, or some noble prospect has opened before you, and especially the quiet ways, where you have walked in sweet converse with your friend-pausing under the trees, drinking at the spring-henceforth they are not the same; a new charm is added; those thoughts spring there perennial, your friend walks there forever."

--John Burroughs, *Elbert Hubbard's Scrapbook*

BTW, the danger these days is not the hiker. Most any deranged person can own a motorized vehicle nowadays. And, from my own experience, anyone hitchhiking on or near a major highway will and/or has been picked up by a State Patrolman or Sheriff's Deputy, background checked on the NCIC (National Crime Information Center) for outstanding warrants or any criminal elements in his/her history and, when determined to be harmless, dropped back off at the on-ramp to the highway and admonished to hitch from that point *not* on the highway itself. Of course, we experienced hitchhikers know that, with only a short walk up the ramp, we are still technically on the ramp but exposed to the bulk of traffic moving down the main highway. So, after waving goodbye to the state patrolman, it's off up the ramp to solicit the next ride.

My advice to the cautious: use discretion when offering a ride on the "blue highways," for those with something to hide will avoid the super highways where the State Patrol will check them out.

You see, when I was nineteen years old, I had occasion to be forced into hitchhiking from almost the southernmost tip of the state of Texas back to my home in the suburbs of Cleveland,

Ohio. It required six full days of rides, walking, heat, and harrowing experiences seared forever into my memory bank. I have long been thankful for those experiences, since recounting them on paper as an English major in college got me the grades I had hoped for.

Bottom line: I have never been harmed or robbed by a driver when hitchhiking, nor by a hitchhiker to whom I've offered a ride–only by those people I encountered in my daily life, and whom I never suspected.

And the price of my offering a ride to the hitchhiker or hiker? How about the benefit of me having a conversant passenger who helps make the ride more enjoyable and appear to go faster, as well as meeting an interesting new human being who appreciates the ride as much as those I once enjoyed.

I think it was some psychologist who said, "90% of what we worry about never comes to pass, and 100% of what comes never even occurred to us." That concept applies to the common fear of picking up hitchhikers and hikers.

So I admonish everyone to quit worrying about the occasional person in need of a ride. I know you may think it risky—but Helen Keller said, "What is life if there is no adventure?" And that came from a lady who was blind and deaf.

SELECTED ATTITUDE CONTROL PROJECTS

THE GREATEST SALESMAN IN THE WORLD, Og Mandino

THE GREATEST MIRACLE IN THE WORLD, Og, Mandino

THE GREATEST SECRET IN THE WORLD, Og Mandino

THE CHRIST COMMISSION, Og Mandino

THE GIFT OF ACABAR, Og Mandino

"SELF RELIANCE," Ralph Waldo Emerson

PSYCHO-CYBERNETICS, Dr. Maxwell Maltz

THE MAGIC OF THINKING BIG, Dr. David Schwartz

MAN'S SEARCH FOR MEANING, Dr. Viktor Frankl

THINK AND GROW RICH, Napolean Hill

GROW RICH WITH PEACE OF MIND, Napolean Hill

SUCCESS THROUGH A POSITIVE MENTAL ATTITUDE, Napolean Hill

YOU CAN WORK YOUR OWN MIRACLES, Napolean Hill

THE PSYCHOLOGY OF WINNING, Dr. Dennis Waitley

THE TEN SEEDS OF GREATNESS, Dr. Dennis Waitley

SEE YOU AT THE TOP, Zig Ziglar

THE POWER OF POSITIVE THINKING, Dr. Norman Vincent Peale

MOVE AHEAD WITH POSSIBLITY THINKING, Dr. Robert Schuller

IN SEARCH OF EXCELLENCE, Thomas Peters and Robert H. Waterman

THE ONE MINUTE MANAGER, Spencer Johnson, M.D. and Kenneth Blanchard, Ph.D.

THE ONE MINUTE SALESPERSON, Spencer Johnson and Kenneth Blanchard, Ph.D.

BELIEVE, by Rich DeVoss (Co-Founder, Amway Corp.)

HOW TO SELL ANYTHING TO ANYBODY, Joe Girard

WHAT TO SAY WHEN YOU TALK TO YOURSELF, Shad Helmstetter

DO WHAT YOU LOVE, THE MONEY WILL FOLLOW: FINDING YOUR RIGHT LIVELIHOOD, Marsha Sinetar

THE HOLY BIBLE

These are just a few of the books and essays that have had a profound effect on my Attitude Control.

For a more complete list of books, essays, poems, audio and video recordings, please feel free to contact this author at his website: BerniePalmatier.com.

SIGNIFICANT QUOTES FROM PEOPLE I'VE KNOWN

Mark Rednick, my employer, mentor and the owner of Sales Consultants of Dallas, Texas:

- ❖ "Your job doesn't owe you job enjoyment; you owe your job 'job enjoyment.'" (This gave me unmitigated permission to exercise my sense of humor when dealing with my clients.)

- ❖ "Never try to get even when you could have been getting ahead." (Important advice whenever the thought of legally suing anyone comes up.)

- ❖ "Being a professional means 'people come to you.'"

- ❖ "Always let money be a fringe benefit of all the fun you're having; if you're having fun you'll do it well, if you do it well the money will take care of itself." (Advice that he gave me as I entered the world of self-employment.)

- ❖ "Which would you rather have: job security or income security? With income security, you don't need a job. Learn all you can about communicating and persuading via the telephone, and you can generate income wherever there is phone near you and one near another person somewhere on the face of the earth." (And given today's modern telecommunications technology and the proliferation of cell phones, texting, and the internet, the vast majority of people in the world are "near a phone.")

- ❖ (He added "…You can lose both legs, one arm, go totally blind, and go deaf in one ear, but as long as one finger, one ear and your tongue are working, you can make a living.")

- ❖ "If you come to work for me, I'll give you plenty of rope (i.e. freedom); you can use it to make yourself a lariat and rope yourself a fortune, or a noose and hang yourself."

- ❖ Worry is debilitating. Concern is healthy. With worry, you're stuck in one place. With concern, you can take action. With action, you can overcome any challenge."

Emeral Lemaster, my late father-in-law, gave his children this advice, and it comes to mind whenever I hear people say regarding their jobs "They don't pay me enough to do…":

- ❖ "Your employer's part of the bargain is whatever amount of compensation you are offered; your part of the bargain is that you give the job one hundred percent of your effort."

Steve Coleman, a former client of mine and owner of the Total Woman health clubs:

- ❖ "Show me a man who retires, and I'll show you a man who didn't enjoy his work."
- ❖ "The world will help you go in whatever direction it thinks you're already headed in."
- ❖ "On the sands of hesitation bleach the bones of countless millions who, at the dawn of victory, sat down to rest and resting…died." (I have often ended my seminars, speeches, and training sessions with this quote. I follow it with the words, "So, no matter how tired you get or how many people say it won't work, if you have the vision, keep the faith, and take one more step toward your goals. Victory could have been right around the corner.")

And a few that stay with me—perhaps they will amuse or resonate with you, as well:

- ❖ **"Life is just a bowl of cherries but it's your responsibility to remove the pits."
- ❖ **"There is no test that will accurately predict exactly when in the future an individual might become inspired to do a 180 degree turnaround–inspired about a product, service, doing their job, or just determined to become NUMBER ONE and closer to irreplaceable." (This is my conclusion regarding profile testing in the hiring process)

Occasionally, when someone thanks me for something that I've done, I repeat this odd colloquialism:

"It was the least I could do. I thought and thought and thought, 'What's the LEAST I could do,' and that was it." (Seems they ought to be offended that I put no effort into thinking what would have been the MOST I could do.)

136

When I say something that exasperates **my wife**, I often say, "I just couldn't resist." She always nails me with:

❖ "You didn't try very hard, did you?"

A **young college student's** advice to his former high school underclassmen regarding depression and the contemplation of suicide:

❖ "Never, never, never a permanent solution to a temporary situation."

Mark Runkle, founder of Midwest Microperipherals/Infotel Distributing and currently developer of Mountain View Meadows in Helena, Montana:

❖ "Success is mainly determined by the inability to give up."

❖ "Focus, focus, focus; we aren't doing anything else until we get our primary function to 100%."

A quote that my favorite high school basketball coach, **Mr. Roland Platz,** had on a plaque over his office door, and that has influenced every athletic and business endeavor that I've ever been involved in:

❖ "It matters not whether you win or lose, but how you played the game."

❖ And three words **my father** could never say, and that I appreciate from all who send my way:

❖ "I love you."

SPECIAL THANKS

The following are the names, in no particular order, of people who had a particular and positive impact on my life. Those of you named will hopefully remember and know why I am recognizing and thanking you. Most of you I can never repay, so I hope my efforts to "pay it forward" have had some success:

- ❖ Mr. Edwin "Bunk" Chapman, my maternal grandfather
- ❖ (Sure wish I could remember some sharing he did one evening while leaning on his cane as I watched the cows in the clover preventing them from getting into the corn.)
- ❖ My favorite quote of his: "I care not a man's color, religion, country of origin; I care only that he be honest."
- ❖ Mrs. Nellie B. Chapman, my maternal grandmother. (She always fed everyone who came to her door.)
- ❖ Wharton H. "Paul" Palmatier, father
- ❖ Hilda I. Chapman Palmatier, mother
- ❖ David E. and Paul A. Palmatier, brothers
- ❖ Carol L. Palmatier Hook, sister
- ❖ Jerry Gard, boyhood best friend
- ❖ Lorene Gard, Jerry's mother
- ❖ Uncle Bernard Chapman, my namesake; my mother's brother
- ❖ My Little League baseball coach in Berea, Ohio
- ❖ Dick Bouman, neighbor & high school/college friend
- ❖ Eric Olson, neighbor & high school friend
- ❖ Norm Thomas, neighbor & high school friend
- ❖ Andy Repjar, high school & college friend
- ❖ Roland "Rollie" Platz, high school basketball coach, mentor, role model

- Dr. Fred Rader
- Jim Criswell
- Every person who picked me up when hitchhiking
- Vesta Morgan
- Georgia Smith
- Julius "Jules" Lukacs
- Margaret Mary Mack; her mother, father and grandmother
- Bill Steele
- Barbara DeCourcelle
- Jim Edens
- Mark & Anita Rednick
- Tony Freeman
- Georgia Fowles
- Sonny Eggleston
- Peggy McCants
- Millie Russell
- Sue Harstine Bowman
- Gary Muratore
- Gary Little
- Danny & Michael Johnson, Attorneys
- David Cantrell
- Sharon Earnshaw
- Henry "Glenn" Lark, cousin
- Maybelle, Marjorie, Eddie Lease, cousins
- Michelle "Shelley" Lehman Cook & parents, William & "Rickie"
- Daniel Austin Palmatier
- Joe Logan

- ❖ Brent McKinley
- ❖ David and Kathy Killiany
- ❖ Mark Runkle & Rebecca Ryland (Runkle)
- ❖ Judy C. Lemaster Palmatier (as always, "My Lovely Bride") & her parents, Emeral & Ruby
- ❖ Trace Andrew Palmatier

Disclaimer: To those of you who remember me and what you did to assist, inform or change me for the better in this life, and whom I have failed to acknowledge here, I will continue wracking my brain to remember you, thank you, and pass your kindness on in hopes of making this world a better place for all mankind.

ABOUT THE AUTHOR

Bernie Palmatier was born. He lived his formative years in a "war project" near Cleveland, Ohio. Therefore, he cannot be blamed for growing up a "project kid," and a fan of the baseball Indians and the football Browns. (You know, "Raise a child up in the way and he will not depart from it". So, someday, the Indians WILL win the World Series and the Browns the Super Bowl. Question: Will Bernie still be alive to witness either?)

He started his career in direct sales with a division of the Reader's Digest while a pre-med student at THE Ohio State University in Columbus, Ohio. Several years as a life and health insurance salesman in El Paso, Texas made him a lover of Mexican food, and gave him an appreciation for both *la corrida* (bullfights–a misnomer), and the motto "*manana*" (the Spanish word for "tomorrow," which explains the paucity of ulcers in that country). He then joined a division of Management Recruiters International (MRI) of Dallas, Texas, called Sales Consultants, where he filled FIFTEEN fee-paid positions in a single month, and achieved the honor of National Recruiter of the Year. He was promoted to Department Head, Assistant Manager, and Manager of the Dallas office. It was there that Bernie learned and became committed to the art of persuasion by telephone.

He started his first business venture in Cleveland, Ohio, and has been involved in start-ups in everything from men's hair care to restaurants to retail stores, to initiating one of the very first Telemarketing Service Bureaus in the U.S. After moving his business to Dayton, Ohio, he ultimately evolved to consulting and training in the art of Tele-Selling, developing a seminar program called "Secrets of Telemarketing" that he has presented all over the country, as well as served as an Adjunct Professor at several colleges and universities.

It was while providing attitude assistance to his staff of TSR's (Telemarketing Sales/Service Representatives) that he first developed his "Attitude Control Program." Since there is no career in the world that requires exposure to such a high incidence of rejection, Bernie found that burnout is truly the bane of the Tele-Sales function, and that prevention of that condition is the only solution to high turnover. (Other seminars that Bernie provides include: "Secrets of TM Supervison," "Humor As A Stress/Success Management Tool," and "Humor for Seniors.")

Bernie felt there needed to be a simple method for raising awareness of the power of Self-Help Psychology. That gave birth to The Grunch Who Ate The Bottom Line! Technology, the internet, eBooks, and Print On Demand (POD) publishing now make it possible to share the message with people throughout the world cost effectively, along with Bernie's motivational system "Attitude Control."

Check out Bernie's website & blog: www.BerniePalmatier.com

Find Bernie on Facebook.

Email him at: **BeautifulDay@woh.rr.com** OR **BeautifulDay1941@gmail.com**

The retention and recall ratios are markedly increased by the meter- and rhyme-factors of jingles in the advertising of products and services. It is the author's hope that you will select the "jingle" in *The Grunch Who Ate The Bottom Line* that will most help to establish your personal "Attitude Control" habit, and convey the message, benefits, and fun of positive thinking to others.

Watch for more books in *The Grunch* series that will explore the parents' role in positive thinking, and the effect of positive thinking on physical health.

Always remember: *"Life is just a bowl of cherries, but it's your responsibility to remove the pits!"*

--ATS Publishing

Made in the USA
Charleston, SC
18 December 2013